Belfast Politics

CLASSICS OF IRISH HISTORY
General Editor: Tom Garvin

Original publication dates of reprinted titles are given in brackets

Belfast Politics

Thoughts on the British Constitution

WILLIAM BRUCE
and HENRY JOY

edited by John Bew

UNIVERSITY COLLEGE DUBLIN PRESS
Preas Choláiste Ollscoile Bhaile Átha Cliath

First published 1794
This abridged edition first published by
University College Dublin Press 2005
© John Bew 2005

ISBN 1 904558–21–6
ISSN 1383–6883

University College Dublin Press
Newman House, 86 St Stephen's Green
Dublin 2, Ireland
www.ucdpress.ie

Cataloguing in Publication data available from
the British Library

Text design by Lyn Davies,
Frome, Somerset, England
Typeset in Ireland in Ehrhardt by
Elaine Burberry, Bantry, Co. Cork
Printed on acid-free paper by Colourbooks, Dublin

CONTENTS

INTRODUCTION

John Bew

BIOGRAPHICAL NOTE

Rev. William Bruce DD (1757–1841), and Henry Joy jun. (1754–1835) were arguably the leading cultural and political heavyweights in Georgian Belfast. Heavily involved in the Society for Promoting Knowledge, the Literary Society and the 1792 Harp Festival, they set the tone for much of Belfast's intellectual life in the decades before and after the Act of Union. Also prominent in the Irish Volunteer movement, both men were believed to be among the most advanced of Ireland's reformers until the early 1790s. As members of the Northern Whig club, they welcomed the French Revolution in the warmest terms and were heavily involved in organising the Bastille Day celebrations which took place in Belfast in 1791 and 1792. As the decade continued, however, they became disillusioned with the radicalisation of the reform movement and the increasingly draconian response of the government. In particular, they were fierce critics of the radical notion that a French invasion would secure any sustainable measure of liberation for Ireland. It was for this reason that they joined the Belfast merchant yeomanry corps – set up to resist insurrection and foreign invasion – just before the outbreak of the 1798 rebellion. They were followed by many other influential local men who reiterated their commitment to Parliamentary reform, their independence from government commission and their reluctance to take up arms against kinsmen and former friends. That Bruce and Joy subsequently became prominent supporters of the Act of Union makes their political progression even more important in understanding the supposed 'transformation' of many Presbyterian radicals from 'rebels to unionists'. *Belfast Politics* provides the keynote to the sense of intellectual continuity among the many who followed a similar path to the authors but have often been labelled political turncoats and reactionaries.[2]

Of the two men, William Bruce occupied the more prominent public role as one of Ireland's leading Unitarian clergymen. In 1790 he left Dublin to become minister of Belfast's prestigious non-subscribing First Presbyterian congregation. In the same year he was also elected principal of the Belfast Academy where he lectured on moral philosophy, classics and history. Unusually for a Dissenter, he was a BA of Trinity College, Dublin – which gave him connections with the Episcopalian ruling elite – and he also studied at the Dissenting Academy in Warrington and Glasgow University. Towards the end of the 1790s Bruce came to think of himself as an 'alarmed Whig'. But as one of the earliest exponents of the secret ballot in the early 1780s, he was at one time regarded as one of the most radical men in the Irish Volunteer movement – a patriotic body which had armed itself to resist potential French invasion in the late 1770s and subsequently became the popular wing of the reform movement.[3] Notably, Bruce's closest friend from childhood had been William Drennan, regarded as the intellectual inspiration behind the United Irishmen. In part, *Belfast Politics* was the product of a very public fallout between the two friends over the latter's increasing radicalism and involvement with that society.[4]

The defining feature of Bruce's political creed derived from the fact that both he and Drennan had been born into a unique radical Ulster Presbyterian patriot tradition, with close links to the Scottish Enlightenment. Their families had been foremost among an influential group of non-subscribing 'new light' (Unitarian) Presbyterians who had been closely tied to the Ulster-born Scottish Enlightenment philosopher Francis Hutcheson and the 'real Whig' theorist Robert Molesworth. Drennan's father had established a school with Hutcheson and Bruce's uncle (Hutcheson's cousin) was a publisher of political and religious tracts such as James Harrington's 1656 republican work, *The Commonwealth of Oceana*, which he reproduced in 1737. This set bequeathed a complex discourse of theological liberalism, classical republicanism and Scottish Enlightenment thinking, which became contested political currency in the upheavals of the 1790s.[5] Despite their ideological divergence from 1791, both Bruce and Drennan were very conscious of their intellectual ancestry and each believed he was doing his utmost to maintain it.

The intimate 'new light' connections by no means precluded involvement in a wider political sphere. There was also a strong connection between the Bruces and the Stewart family of County Down.[6] In 1790, the young Robert Stewart – later Lord Castlereagh – had been the great hope of local reformers when he was elected to the Irish Parliament. Although Castlereagh subsequently became a political enemy because of his prominent role in the military censure of Ulster, Bruce was able to use this connection to negotiate favourable terms for the Presbyterian community in the passing of the Act of Union. A key figure behind these wider political connections was another 'new light' man, veteran Belfast physician and reformer Dr Alexander Haliday (1728–1802), 'a Genuine Whig . . . nurtured in the philosophy of Hutcheson' and 'the principles of civil and religious liberty'.[7] Haliday, who drew up the resolutions of the Northern Whig club, was respected across the political spectrum in Belfast but he is chiefly known for his friendship with the 'Volunteer Earl', Lord Charlemont. The Belfast moderates should not be identified too closely with the political convictions of Charlemont; they were sometimes too precipitate and too radical for his brand of aristocratic Whiggism.[8] Nevertheless, by dedicating *Belfast Politics* to Haliday and Charlemont, the authors were clearly emphasising their attachment to an older, long-established reform cause.

Henry Joy jun. also had an established position in Ulster's political elite; he was a cousin of the celebrated United Irish martyr Henry Joy McCracken, hanged in 1798. The Joys, of Hugenot ancestry, had been Belfast's leading family in philanthropy, business and Volunteer politics for nearly half a century. Yet, while the story of Henry Joy McCracken is etched onto popular historical consciousness in Ireland, the reality is that Henry Joy jun. was the more influential man in contemporary Belfast. In 1790 he took over sole proprietorship and editorship of the newspaper his family had established in 1737, the *Belfast News-Letter*.[9] In the 1790s it took up a position which was critical of the increasingly radical organ of the United Irishmen, the *Northern Star*, while remaining faithful to the old Volunteer cause.[10] Although Henry Joy sold the paper in 1795, he continued to write in it to express his exasperation at the course of the French Revolution, particularly the continued suspension of the Revolutionary constitution. Joy's *Historical Collections* of 1817 intended to vindicate the course taken by the Belfast moderate Whigs in the 1790s; so while it was unapologetically unionist, it blamed the interference of foreign states for 'goading' the French Revolutionary project 'into madness' and identified closely with the revival of the British Parliamentary reform movement.[11]

Bruce, as a distinguished classical scholar and writer, seems to have been the dominant influence on the political essays of *Belfast Politics*. Nevertheless, there is strong evidence for suggesting that

Henry Joy – who compiled the work and probably wrote the preface – had a significant impact on the content and style of the collection. He was certainly a distinguished writer and political strategist in his own right. His private papers convey his familiarity with an eclectic group of both classical and Enlightenment authorities – Pliny, Milton, Gibbon, Robert Burns, Arthur Young, Dr Johnson, and the Edinburgh University moral philosopher Dugald Stewart – some of which can be detected in *Belfast Politics*. More importantly, as secretary to the Belfast Volunteers, he was the chief agent of the links forged by the Volunteers in the 1780s with Parliamentary reform movements across the British Isles, an aspect of late eighteenth-century Irish patriotism which is often ignored. The Joy manuscripts, in themselves a case for a 'new British history', contain a fertile correspondence with prominent Irish and British reformers from Henry Grattan and Lord Charlemont to Major Cartwright, Richard Price and Christopher Wyvill of the Yorkshire Association.[12] If analysis of late eighteenth-century patriotism is restricted to Ireland or mainland Britain as separate cases, we lose sight of the fact that the course followed by men such as Bruce and Joy had clear parallels in British reform politics.[13]

In fact, the political orbit of the Belfast moderates extended even beyond the parameters of British politics. Notably, as vociferous supporters of the American Revolution, they were avid observers of American attitudes to Revolutionary France. Visiting Bath in 1800, Joy discussed these issues with Dr Archibald Maclaine, an old Belfast Whig, student of Hutcheson and a former classmate of Adam Smith at Glasgow. Maclaine had been an emissary of the Scottish Church at the Hague for much of the second half of the century before he had left in 1796, fearing the consequences of French invasion. He reported to Joy a conversation he claimed to have had with John Adams, American minister to the United Provinces in the early 1780s and from 1797, the second American

President. Adams had reiterated the argument that the American
Revolution had been fought in defence of the 'unrivalled Excellence
of the British Constitution'. Other forms of government 'company
it to the rock of Gib[raltar]', so Adams was supposed to have said,
but only the British could navigate around it as 'the waves often
foam and roar . . . its Foundations Entire'.[14]

Those involved in the politics of Belfast thus found themselves
grappling with debates and ideas that were by no means isolated to
the confines of the local political scene. When Joy heard this
account of Maclaine's meeting with Adams, Napoleonic France
was at the height of its powers, Ireland was recovering from a
rebellion and the Act of Union was being implemented. At the same
time, Adams was resisting Painite and French-inspired opposition
to his Presidency in America. The prominent involvement of many
United Irishmen – exiled from Ireland in the late 1790s – in Adams's
subsequent defeat, is a potent demonstration of how the political
disputes which afflicted late eighteenth-century Ireland echoed
across the Atlantic world.[15] So if Bruce is seen primarily as the
exponent of a unique Ulster political heritage, it seems that Joy was
equally concerned for the survival of a more widely shared British-
born discourse of constitutionalism. These notions had inspired
support for the American Revolution and they by no means precluded support for the French; but they did provide the ultimate
criteria by which subsequent developments after 1789 were judged.[16]

BELFAST POLITICS REVISITED: 'MODERATION – NONSENSE'

The effect of the French Revolution on this political world was
to galvanise a reform movement that believed it had already
experienced 'Enlightenment', encompassing Scottish and English,
European and transatlantic experience. It should be said that the

sheer diversity of these intellectual influences has been successfully acknowledged in some excellent recent work on the 'twisted roots' of late eighteenth-century Irish patriotism.[17] Nevertheless, the extent to which such notions were hotly disputed concepts *within* the patriot tradition is one theme that could be developed more fully. Significantly, for all the recent revival in interest in Irish radicalism and late eighteenth century political thought, *Belfast Politics* remains a remarkably understudied, overlooked and under-valued work. R. R. Madden, the nineteenth-century historian of the United Irishman, hinted at its significance as 'one of the earliest and most able expositions of arguments in detail in favour of reform to be dealt with'.[18] Ian McBride has since offered a valuable if brief synopsis of its content but as yet there exists no systematic attempt to engage with its arguments in any detail.[19] Some of the best recent major collections on Irish political thought completely fail to mention it.[20]

At first glance, it is tempting to attribute this oversight to something intrinsic to the nature of Irish historical writing on the 1790s. One eloquent but controversial 'revisionist' argument is that the 'progressive' and 'modern' views of the United Irishman have been 'fictionalised and poeticised' by historians out of all proportion to their actual influence at the time.[21] But it does not take a revisionist to make the point, as one of the foremost historians of the United Irishmen has conceded, that 'a preoccupation' with radicals and revolutionaries 'has obscured the diversity of popular politics'.[22] Arguably, the failure to subject wider political opinion – particularly the moderate Whig position in Ulster – to sustained and rigorous analysis is one of the most obvious symptoms of this preoccupation.[23] Furthermore, there is a specific reason for applying this argument to the case of *Belfast Politics*. Significantly, the dismissive verdict on the politics of moderation in Ulster was first delivered by Theobald Wolfe Tone, the revolutionary separatist

figurehead of the United Irishmen, who was instrumental in bringing about the attempted French invasion of Ireland, before he was
captured and killed himself in the custody of British troops. As
James Quinn has argued recently, more than any other figure, Tone
remains a 'legend' in Irish history and his writings (public and
private) have an unparalleled influence on existing commentary on
the 1790s. Notably then, in Tone's journals, the 'Belfast Whigs
seem to have fared particularly badly'.[24]

Crucially, the initial source of tension between Tone and the
Belfast Whigs was one of the most important and most emotive
issues in late eighteenth–century and early nineteenth–century Irish
and British politics: the Catholic question. Tone's brilliant *Argument
on Behalf of the Catholics of Ireland* (1791) had made a huge
intellectual impact in the North of Ireland. Styling himself as a
'Northern Whig', his pamphlet was primarily a plea to Ulster's
liberal Dissenters to embrace fully the cause of Catholic emancipation as the basis of a powerful political alliance with Irish Catholics.
In a series of public meetings and votes in 1791–2, a clear majority
of Belfast reformers were carried over to Tone's position of 'Reform
and the Catholics'.[25] However, when divisions over this question
first emerged in the reform movement in late 1791, Tone – who
believed this was a crucial issue of natural right as well as political
strategy – seized on the hesitancy of Bruce, Joy, Haliday and their
followers to incorporate an 'immediate' emancipation of Roman
Catholics into the reform agenda of the Volunteers. The moderates
also claimed to share a desire to see the repeal of all penal restrictions. But this came with the controversial and somewhat ambiguous
caveat that the process of emancipation should take place '*from time
to time, and as speedily as the circumstances of the country and the
general welfare of the whole kingdom will permit*'.[26] After an argument
on the issue in Belfast, Tone labelled Bruce an 'intolerant high
priest'. Joy, who had actually proposed Tone as a member of the

Northern Whig Club, was a 'cur'. 'Moderation', for Tone 'was nonsense' and the arguments of the moderates 'All hollow'. Amusingly, Tone afterwards reflected on the stupidity of arguing over wine. But it is his account that still dominates modern historical understanding of the dispute. Thus moderate reservations, to borrow a phrase from Bartlett's introduction to Tone's journals, are bracketed as 'atavistic'. Although not quite 'ignorant backwoodsmen', we are told, it is 'clear that the Enlightenment had still some way to go among the middle classes of Belfast'.[27]

Given its importance, it is tempting to take the Catholic question as the only yardstick by which the relative political 'advancement' of putative liberals in late eighteenth-century Ireland is measured. But any attempt to divide the political players of the 1790s into the enlightened or unenlightened obscures the complexity and disjointedness of the political scene; for instance, while Bruce's position was unclear, Joy saw the 1793 Catholic Relief Act as consistent with his gradualist position and called for further measures in 1795.[28] Indeed, exactly what sort of 'Enlightenment' occurred in the late eighteenth century and how far it permeated Ireland beyond the radical vanguards in Belfast and Dublin are in themselves matters of intense academic debate.[29] In some areas – notably rural Armagh, suffering from tensions in the linen industry – the previous few years had seen the emergence of unprecedented levels of religious strife. If anything, as one letter in Bruce's papers confirms, the self-image of liberal Presbyterians and Volunteers was of a moderate bulwark standing between rival Episcopalian and Catholic factions.[30] Of course, however much they stressed these wider concerns, Bruce and Joy's position on this issue cost them much of their influence at the head of the reform movement. Nonetheless, the Catholic question was not the only boundary of political identification or the basis of an irreparable split within that movement. Tone may have argued this; others, better acquainted with the

Ulster political scene, such as Drennan, believed that it was very much a secondary factor in the growing schism between moderate and radical reformers.[31]

Disputes about the relative merits of political gradualism had been a pervasive feature of political life across a whole range of issues since the early 1780s. The problem for the moderates, which Haliday quickly identified after meeting Tone in 1791, was that it suited the radicals to emphasise the Catholic issue in order to portray their opponents as 'men of little mind'.[32] This was all the more galling because the moderates felt it reduced a disparate set of concerns to a single area of contention. Before the 1792 Bastille Day celebrations in Belfast, rumours had been circulating that Tone was coming to Belfast to 'force seditious papers down their throats'. Bartlett has argued convincingly that he was already a committed separatist and republican by this stage and there was undoubtedly a suspicion that the radical agenda extended well beyond Catholic emancipation and Parliamentary reform.[33] The correspondence between Bruce and William Drennan reveals that there was a growing tension between those committed to reform by constitutional means and those who thought a more revolutionary measure necessary from the mid-1780s.[34] The most famous symbol of this radicalisation took place in early 1793 when Belfast's radical newspaper, the *Northern Star*, dropped the Crown which had appeared above the Irish harp on its emblem. This ostensibly disloyal gesture has become something of a cliché for the historians of the period, but the fact that it was highlighted by Joy in his private manuscripts demonstrates just how potent this symbol was.[35]

Belfast Politics is best seen as an attempt to disentangle the Catholic issue from what the moderates saw as much graver concerns and more divisive issues: the increasingly revolutionary and separatist rhetoric of the radicals, particularly talk of a possible French 'liberation', and the resultant intensification of government reaction.

Although Bruce and Joy acknowledged that they had lost much of their influence on Belfast's radical majority, they were confident that, in this case, they were intervening on much firmer political ground. For all the radicalism of the embryonic revolutionary elites of Belfast and Dublin, it should not be assumed that radical influence on the rest of the reform movement went unchallenged. Admittedly, in some areas, the reach of the United Irishmen was already formidable.[36] But when *Belfast Politics* was being written, the mood of many of those in the Ulster reform movement was more sympathetic to the moderate agenda. Much to the frustration of the radicals, the resolutions of the 1793 Volunteer Convention at Dungannon included a firm commitment to the constitution and the connection with Britain, a rejection of republican principles as applied to Ireland and criticism of the regicide in France.[37] While the *Northern Star* brashly asserted that the Convention had shown that 'the whole province is one great society of United Irishmen', privately its editor complained that the meeting had been 'rather led by aristocracy'.[38] Notably, more conservative elements in the Volunteers – such as Joseph Pollock of Newry, who demanded a firmer commitment to the constitution – complained about Joy's personal dominance over the proceedings in his capacity as 'Delegate, Committee-man, Secretary, Printer and Historiographer to the Convention'.[39] Writing to Charlemont, Joy confidently concluded that the Convention 'decides the opinion of Ulster on some essential points'.[40]

'THOUGHTS ON THE BRITISH CONSTITUTION'

It was not then from a particularly marginalised or reactionary standpoint that Bruce and Joy embarked upon the series of essays which comprise this edition of *Belfast Politics*. 'Thoughts on the British Constitution' was a collection of twenty articles, most of which were originally printed in the *News-Letter* from late 1792 and throughout 1793. They challenged the increasingly polarised political stances taken up by both the government and the most radical reformers during this period. Although they were often written in response to particular political events, the authors believe they constituted a logical series of essays with a cohesive theme (see note on the text).

If historians have largely missed the significance of the essays, this was not the case with contemporaries from across the political spectrum. Even radicals such as William Drennan, described them 'as good as any Thoughts on the subject can be'.[41] His sister, Martha McTier – who also believed they were 'very well wrote, particularly to convince and please the lower ranks' – revealed that some United Irishmen had considered reprinting the essays before 'mean motives' against Bruce and Joy intervened. Significantly, she also reported that 'the aristocracy are more angry than any others' at the work; the Marquess of Downshire – a local Tory landlord – 'prefers the [*Northern*] *Star* as an open enemy'.[42] Lord Charlemont, to whom the 'Thoughts' were dedicated, assured Joy that the collection, 'in an historical view, well deserves to be remembered'. But he also doubted whether publication was advisable in the current climate, despite the fact that the authors had not put their name to the text and that many of the essays had already been published. 'The Book', he promised, 'is under lock and key and shall be seen by no one'.[43] In the event, after only eighty copies were printed, the authors abandoned publication for fear of government recrimination.[44]

The first complaint of the moderates was against the Irish administration in Dublin Castle. 'If the Government were as wise as it is strong', Joy complained, 'having shown its power, it would next aim at conciliation instead of exasperation'.[45] But the authors were equally resolute in rejecting radical republican solutions to Ireland's political paralysis. 'The general idea of the thoughts', Joy reassured Charlemont on the publication of *Belfast Politics* in late spring 1794, 'was to excite a veneration of the constitution in the breasts of the multitude'.[46] Rejection of the *status quo* was not to be equated with rejection of the British constitution and the whole basis of British political life. The continued failure of the post-revolutionary French governments to produce a stable constitutional settlement merely strengthened this conviction. Talk of a French-assisted rebellion was not only utopian in the eyes of the moderates, it was a betrayal of the founding principles of the reform movement. The real aim of these polemical articles was to challenge the presumptions of radical republicans and separatists on the terms of their own discourse and to demonstrate that the authors felt just as comfortable on 'Enlightenment' terrain.

To this end, the first thing that is striking about the text is that it acts as a corrective to the common assumption that the 1790s were dominated by the debate between Paine and Burke. While the impact of *Rights of Man* was undoubtedly significant, it was not quite, as Tone would have it, the 'Koran' of Belfast.[47] Indeed, even among radicals, Paine's initial popularity in Belfast was severely dented by the subsequent publication of his *Age of Reason* in 1794. Bruce's assault on Paine in a series of sermons that year proved so popular that they were attended by 'an immense crowd' of United Irishmen who joined in the 'general praise'.[48] At the same time, it did not follow that in rejecting elements of Paine, the Belfast moderates were increasingly 'following the reasoning of Edmund Burke'.[49] Having been a great supporter of his writings on American independence, in 1790 the *News-Letter* had dismissed Burke's critique of the French Revolution as the 'melancholy proofs of a great mind on the wane'.[50]

More importantly, regardless of his views on France, Burke cut an increasingly problematic figure to Presbyterian reformers during the early 1790s. For example, his *Letter to Sir Hercules*

Langrishe, which attacked Irish Dissenters for making 'seditious propositions to the Catholics' – had already contributed to an ugly dispute between Catholic and Protestant members of the Dublin Society of United Irishmen.[51] Notably, the first essay of 'Thoughts on the British Constitution' ended with an explicit complaint that an obsession with the Burke–Paine debate had restricted the parameters of debate. It consciously distanced itself from both 'an absurd veneration of ancient establishments, which borders on folly and superstition' and 'a hardy contempt of the experience of ages, an inordinate love of veneration, and a desire of *destroying* where we might *repair*'. 'Whether two living characters', they wrote, 'whose books furnish the conversation of the present day have sat for these portraits – the reader must determine'.

Belfast Politics is firmly grounded in a much richer tradition of pre-1789 British and European Enlightenment thought. 'Far from me and my Friends', ran a quotation attributed to Dr Johnson in Joy's journal for 1797, 'be such frigid Philosophy, as may enable us to walk unmoved over any Ground that has been consecrated by Wisdom, Leaning and Virtue'.[52] But it was one thing to appeal to precedent and history against abstract principle and notions of universal right, and quite another to 'follow the reasoning of Burke'. Bruce and Joy drew on a much more diverse and radical indigenous British constitutional discourse. In fact, the most recurrent themes in the text are notions which had been crucial to the intellectual foundations of the Volunteers for many years: the importance of a virtuous and active citizenry, the underlying notion of a polemic between 'liberty' and 'corruption' and an emphasis on the popular, or 'republican', part of the constitution. Demonstrating a strong familiarity with the works of Machiavelli (drawn on directly at the end of the preface), many of the essays are more markedly evocative of the classical republican or civic humanist tradition, generally thought to be the preserve of the United

Irishmen. It was to these notions – transmitted through the work of men like Francis Hutcheson and John Toland – that the authors turned for what they believed were the foundation stones of citizenship and commonwealth.[53]

Notionally, the use of these radical, potentially revolutionary authorities for a politically moderate agenda seems to present a paradox. As Small has accurately asserted, at the heart of classical republican theory was the right to revolution in the last resort. For Curtin also, this 'represented the union of republican theory and practice' and it is true many radicals who rebelled in 1798 defended their actions precisely by recourse to such doctrine.[54] However, there are two qualifications to be made. First, as Worden has described, much of the seventeenth-century republicanism of men such as James Harrington and Algernon Sidney became redirected away from anti-monarchism and incorporated into mainstream Whig discourse in the following century.[55] Second, Bruce believed that the use of these authorities, particularly by those radicals who were mooting an alliance with the French, was not always entirely consistent with the original doctrines. From Machiavelli to Sidney, the right to revolution was held up as a means of returning to 'first principles'. Revolution was used in the classical astronomical sense of a circular motion, a rotation to a former position or a restoration of lawful authority, rather than the more recent French Revolutionary idea of a forcible breach with the past: an idea increasingly attractive to the most radical elements in Irish politics.[56] For the moderates, if the radicals were prepared to abandon precedent and to welcome in an invading army, they were not returning to the first principles of the constitution but ripping up its very foundations. Patriotism moreover, by these authorities, could never be the sole preserve of a revolutionary cabal and liberty could never be delivered by foreign troops. At the core of 'Thoughts on the British Constitution' is the notion of reform as 'restoration'. As such, it reasserted the place of the Irish reform movement within the existing 'constitutionalist idiom'.[57]

It is also necessary to be precise about the nature of the 1790s 'republicanism' which *Belfast Politics* sets out to counteract. First, the term underwent something of a transformation of meaning during this decade. The French Revolution confounded even Rousseau's dictum that a republic could only exist in small units such as a city-state.[58] At the same time, among many Irish radicals, there was a shift from a traditional attachment to the 'spirit' of republican government to the precise 'form' (see Essay No. VIII). The authors of *Belfast Politics* maintained this attachment to the 'spirit' of the republican government. On the other hand, United Irish propaganda began to draw a connection between a fully demo-cratic state – without aristocracy and King – and a republic.[59] This democratic reading was, however, in many ways a perversion of the classical republicanism of the seventeenth century, often described as a 'language' rather than a 'programme', defining itself 'in relation not to constitutional structures but moral principles'.[60] Rather than stipulate any precise form of constitutional arrangement, the primary criteria of any governmental system was that it secured the common will, the public good and virtue: a notion by no means irreconcilable with monarchy and aristocracy (see Nos VIII and XVIII). Indeed, one enduring subtlety of this tradition, scarcely acknowledged in United Irish propaganda, was its rejection of the purely democratic and unstable city-states of Ancient Greece: hence the attempt of the authors to draw similarities between the ancient Athenian and modern French systems of government (No. XVI).[61] Thus, for all their professed flexibility over the precise terms of any future Parliamentary reform, the authors of *Belfast Politics* completely rejected universal manhood suffrage (see Nos IX to XII).

'Thoughts on the British Constitution' was therefore following an established, if momentarily unfashionable, path in reconciling these civic humanist traditions with Polybius, the major classical authority on mixed, balanced government (No. VI).[62] Admittedly, many committed Irish republicans became impatient with the celebrated checks and balances of the British constitution as 'more conversant in the constitution of a clock than a commonwealth'.[63] But it is important to understand that there was an alternative view that there was nothing inherent in the British system of government which prevented the eventual attainment of these civic humanist aspirations. By this stage, the authors were acquainted with the work of future American President John Adams, whose American essays in response to Paine had been printed for the first time in Dublin in 1793.[64] What they shared with Adams – and many others in the Atlantic political world who were imbued with seventeenth-century classical republican discourse – was an alarm at the new brand of radicalism extolled by men such as Paine, William Godwin and Henry Yorke. This placed an unprecedented value on human reason and rejected the prevailing political obsession with checks and balances as a mask for corruption and special interests.[65]

A NATIONALIST OR A UNIONIST TEXT?

Belfast Politics enriches our understanding of political thought in late eighteenth-century Britain and Ireland. Quite how much its significance goes beyond that is a matter of contention. Over the last two hundred years there have been two re-editions of the text, both of which aim to place the work in very different traditions. In 1818, the Belfast-based journalist John Lawless reproduced the work and added his own introduction.[66] Lawless, a radical agent of O'Connell's Catholic Association and a prominent early nationalist, was attempting to reawaken interest in the patriot tradition in Ulster, which lay largely dormant in the aftermath of the failed rebellion of 1798. He believed that this text captured the Ulster patriot tradition more effectively than any other. But Joy and Bruce, by now strong unionists, objected to his attempt to attach their work to a nationalist agenda which they believed was premised on a very different basis from that in which they had been involved. For many former Ulster patriots, post-Union nationalism seemed to have at its core the notion of the peculiarity of Ireland: a peculiarity increasingly defined by religious difference. 'Thoughts on the British Constitution' had been born of a more traditional agenda which consciously placed itself at the heart of a British Parliamentary reform tradition and stressed the centrality of Irish (often specifically Presbyterian) experience to British political culture and constitutional history.

The paradoxical nature of the book's legacy is further demonstrated by the source of the second re-edition: a 1974 pamphlet by the British and Irish Communist Association (B&ICO). Situating the work in an entirely different bracket, this claimed that the authors 'developed the substance of the liberal unionist position and gave it a very coherent expression'. Although 'only a minority supported that position in 1792–3', it continued, 'the important thing is that it was well-established in speculative politics'.[67] Again, to a certain extent this interpretation also reflects an editorial agenda above the authors' original aim: in this case B&ICO's quasi-unionist leanings of the 1970s. The fact is that Bruce and Joy were writing at a time of great uncertainty; while the idea of a Union was not in itself novel, it had not really permeated mainstream political consciousness as a viable solution to Ireland's problems in the early 1790s.[68] Furthermore, a central assumption of the Volunteer movement had always been that the logical outcome of Parliamentary reform and full enjoyment of the British constitution would be greater levels of Irish legislative independence, albeit within the British connection. Nevertheless, the B&ICO edition undoubtedly detects something which Lawless was unwilling to countenance: a crucial continuity between the late eighteenth century Irish reform movement and early unionist political culture.

The key to comprehending this continuity is to understand is that there was so much more at stake than a purely 'Irish question' in the 1790s. It is easy to underestimate the extent to which the prospect of prolonged war from 1793 between Revolutionary France and Britain completely transformed the European political landscape. In 1779, one prominent patriot writer had been able to point to the independent and strong states of the Swiss and the Dutch, as an inspiration for the Irish to assert their rights as nation.[69] By 1793 the same writer was at pains to argue that the prospect of French dominance over small and weakened states in Europe had fundamentally altered the context in which Irish patriotism had to operate.[70] Lord Castlereagh had also attempted to convince Haliday that if Ireland were to achieve anything like a 'State of Separation' from Britain, it would soon find itself in a 'State of Nature' in European power politics:

> The language of Reason of enlarged and enlightened Policy has not yet permeated thoroughly the Cabinets of Princes. Power and Importance is necessary almost to procure a hearing. I am afraid we should cut a sorry figure and exhibit an appearance not very imposing, were we to appear before them simply clad in the part of our own Insular Dignity and abstracted Freedom . . . it is absurd and romantick to imagine that we can exist for any length of time as a separate and independent state. Where is the successor to Great Britain if we detach ourselves from her? Is it France? That Pile of Ruins! That Melancholy example of misapplied Philosophy, of Political Experiment and Popular Delirium![71]

Was this the best time, Castlereagh asked, to 'tear asunder the ties of Interest, Affection, Blood, Constitution, every thing nearest to our hearts, and dearest to our senses which unite us to Britain?'[72]

Belfast Politics became the reference point for the significant body of opinion that refused to follow Castlereagh's political path yet was not immune to these wider concerns of realpolitik. Thus Haliday still bitterly complained that Castlereagh was 'Pitt-ized with a vengeance . . . wanting to proselyte me, which was surely not worth his pains'.[73] But years before Castlereagh presented the Act of Union to the Irish Parliament in 1799, there was an increasing realisation among many former Volunteers that, for the immediate future, the choice that had to be made was not between Ireland and Britain, but Britain and France.[74] It was for this reason that the Belfast Whigs were eager to remind their readers that it was the British constitution that had been the prized political system of the European Enlightenment. As the first essay of the series insisted, what better vindications of it were there than the writings of Millar, Montesquieu, Voltaire and Rousseau? Between them, these writers had celebrated its amenability to change and improvement and the 'republican' balance between Crown, aristocracy and democracy. Moreover, what was the American constitution but 'a declaration in writing of the most primary principles of that very British one'? (No. VII)

It is true, as contemporaries realised and historians have noted since, that appeals to 'the constitution' were often the first port of call for radicals and reactionaries alike.[75] But 'Thoughts on the British Constitution' transcended unspecific or flimsy attachment to rhetoric by also displaying a general confidence in the direction of progress and pace of change in the British polity, however slow and stuttering that sometimes appeared in Ireland (Nos XVII–XX). It was by no means a perfect constitution and there was nothing particularly romantic about the way in which it had functioned and developed. In the graphic classical similes used by the authors, it resembled Hydra, the many-headed mythical beast or Antaeus, the wrestler who grew stronger every time he was thrown to the ground (see No. XVIII). The authors shared Hume's realistic 'appreciation of the role of contingency' in its development.[76]

An inevitable corollary of these seismic geopolitical shifts, therefore, was a reappraisal of Irish attitudes to Britain and British identity. Bruce and Joy made no explicit departure from the traditional Irish patriot version of history and its heroes: Molyneux, Swift, Flood and Grattan (Nos XIX and XX). Crucially however, the combination of the fear of invasion and the Francophile tone of domestic radicalism also served to bring out the latent 'British' flavour of reform discourse in the text. Thus, the authors went out of their way to reassert the peculiarity of wider 'British' experience. The introduction of the term 'Britons', used pointedly in the opening quotation from Bolingbroke, was a significant innovation; Bolingbroke may have been an unusual authority for Irish patriot writing but as David Armitage has shown, his work was crucial in the genesis of a form of Whig patriotism in Britain during this period.[77]

This rhetorical innovation should not be confused in any way with a rejection of Irish identity. Rather, the label of 'Britons' – a disputed term from mid-century – was generally used to refer to the non-Saxon peoples at the margins of the British Isles. As Colin Kidd has described in the case of Scotland, this meant that it proved a useful instrument in the construction of 'a more inclusive and properly British' notion of the polity, which 'aspired towards full British participation in English liberties'.[78] Even at the height of its popularity, the French Revolution had been regarded as a specifically 'Gallic' achievement. Progress and change did not simply come though the application of human wisdom and the Revolution had no abstract quality which was directly transportable into a British or Irish arena. By contrast, for authors of *Belfast*

Politics, the British Constitution was 'so admirably suited to our situation, our habits, and our wishes', something highly reminiscent of Montesquieu's notion of the 'spirit'.[79] As Scottish Enlightenment philosophers such as Millar and Ferguson had also argued, existing political institutions and governmental forms were moulded by the peculiarities of national history and development, especially the social or economic base of a particular society.[80] Bruce and Joy identified strongly with these peculiarities.

Belfast Politics therefore articulated an idea of 'Britishness' that was defined primarily by reference to polity, history and the socio-economic basis of society. Admittedly, as regards local experience, central to the self-image of Irish Presbyterians was the notion that their political culture and historical role in the seventeenth century made them intrinsic to the constitution, perhaps even the 'fathers' of it.[81] Nevertheless, 'Britons' was used in a sense broader than any narrow definition of race, religion or contemporary anti-French sentiment. The identification with Britain articulated in *Belfast Politics* is made to counteract the Francophile leanings of some radicals and separatists, while remaining loose enough not to contradict Irish patriot demands. In fact, the more expansive the definition, and the less it relied on exclusive notions such as ancient 'Saxon' liberties, the stronger the case for full enjoyment of the British Constitution.[82] As described in a quote from John Millar which opens essay No. I, this Constitution is 'the only one in the annals of mankind that has aimed at the diffusion of liberty through a multitude of People, spread over a wide extent of territory'; it was inextricably linked to the manners, history and 'spirit' of all the peoples and races of the two islands. *Belfast Politics* is far from a unionist text but it provides a crucial insight into the complexities of identity and nationality in late eighteenth-century Ireland. At the very least, it does enough to suggest that the sub-sequent emergence of unionist or British sentiment among so many late eighteenth-century Irish patriots may have had surer foundations than simple, elemental political reaction, Evangelical Protestantism and a wholesale 'transformation' of principles.

ACKNOWLEDGEMENTS

For their help and advice with this introduction I would like to thank Dr Brendan Simms, Dr Jon Parry, Dr Tony Stewart, Dr Ian McBride, Professor Tom Bartlett and Dr Colin Kidd. Dr Patrick Maume and Dr Michael Brown were kind enough to read a draft of the whole edition and they both made very helpful suggestions. John Gray, at the Linenhall library, also went out of his way to assist me. Finally, I must thank Barbara Mennell at UCD Press for her enthusiastic support.

For the purposes of publication, it has been necessary to exclude a significant section of the original edition of *Belfast Politics*. Much of the first edition was taken up with a chronicle of the 'Debates, Resolutions, and Narratives' of the main political meetings of Belfast and Ulster reformers from the early 1790s, featuring Belfast United Irishmen, the Northern Whig club, Ulster Volunteer Corps, the Belfast Reading Society and local Roman Catholic associations. These have been removed with the small section at the start of the original preface, which referred to these proceedings. Also removed is a report of the public meetings on the Catholic question in Belfast; though it should be noted that the authors summarised their position in the preface and this is subject to further critical analysis in the notes. It has also been necessary to take out the reproduction of the newspaper dispute between Bruce and William Drennan over the oath taken by prospective United Irishmen.[1]

It is hoped that neither the main essence of the original work nor its impact should be overly diminished by this. Bruce and Joy's aim in including all these resolutions and debates was to allay the impression that they had given a partial account of the town's politics and to emphasise that they were not misrepresenting the events which had taken place. The contention of this edition is that 'Thoughts on the British Constitution' stands as a crucial work of political theory in its own right, worthy of reproduction as a separate treatise.

Of the twenty essays, most appeared in the *Belfast News-Letter* from late 1792 to late 1793. It should be noted that the demands of newspaper publication dictated the style and length of the essays. At various stages the authors reflect that the restrictions of space preclude the discussion of certain points and it is clear from studying the original copies, that the essays were sometimes rushed or postponed in response to important political events. Although the essays are quite cohesive, the occasionality of each must be emphasised; the authors were often responding to dramatic events in domestic and European politics. Accordingly, a brief account of the immediate context of each is given in explanatory notes at the top of each Number. The authors also made some changes to the order in which the 'Thoughts' first appeared and later added essays which did not appear in the original news-paper series (these are undated in the text). In some instances, they also used footnotes which have been preserved in this edition. Where production deviated from the original newspaper format, this is explained in the notes. The editor has tried to be as faithful as possible to the original sense of the work. Obvious errors have been removed but the structure, punctuation, grammar and idiosyncratic spelling of the original text have been largely preserved as they appeared in the 1794 edition. Square brackets [ ] used in the text of *Belfast Politics* are those of Bruce and Joy. The editor's comments have been set in curly brackets { }.

BELFAST POLITICS:

OR,

A COLLECTION

OF THE DEBATES, RESOLUTIONS,

AND

OTHER PROCEEDINGS OF THAT TOWN,

IN THE YEARS

M,DCC,XCII, AND M,DCC,XCIII.

WITH

STRICTURES ON THE TEST

OF CERTAIN OF

THE SOCIETIES OF UNITED IRISHMEN:

ALSO,

THOUGHTS

ON

The Britiſh Conſtitution.

HE KNOWS NOTHING OF MEN, WHO EXPECTS TO CONVINCE
A DETERMINED PARTY MAN; AND HE, NOTHING OF THE
WORLD, WHO DESPAIRS OF THE FINAL IMPARTIALITY OF
THE PUBLIC. *Lavater.*

Note to facsimile of the title page overleaf

Johann Kaspar Lavater (1741–*c*.1801), Swiss theologian and poet. Founder of physiognomics. Pastor in St Peter's Church in Zurich. Deported to Basel because of his protest against the violence of the French Directory.

PREFACE

The distinguished part, which Belfast has always taken in Irish Politics, especially since the beginning of SEVENTEEN HUNDRED AND NINETY TWO, with the applause and condemnation which it has drawn from different parties, suggested the idea of the following collection.

It occurred to the compiler[1] that a faithful report of the proceedings of that town, and the sentiments of those who took a lead in the controversies by which it was agitated, might prove a valuable record. He conceived, that an impartial collection of this kind must be acceptable to all parties; and even indulged the hope that such a review would tend to heal, rather than irritate the wounds, which public intercourse or private friendship might have received during the contest: At all events, he thought he should induce the inhabitants of a town, long conspicuous for harmony, to make a liberal allowance for diversity of sentiment in future, and to hold the right of private judgment as sacred in others as in themselves. To them, it must afford sensible pleasure, and useful entertainment, to contemplate the progress of measures in which they were, individually and collectively, so deeply engaged {. . .} Those who condemned them all, may learn to think more favourably of their intentions and exertions. The advocates for the

MAJORITY, will triumph in the immediate success of its operations. The partisans of the MINORITY, will lament by anticipation
the eventual consequences of premature and precipitate measures;
and find consolation by applauding the sagacity, with which they
foresaw the degradation of the town, and the delusion of the kingdom: while the dispassionate philosopher and practical politician
may trace the progress of popular ardour, and the operation of
those minute springs which often produce the most important
movements, in the political machine {...}[2]

These are followed by a series of papers, entitled, THOUGHTS
ON THE BRITISH CONSTITUTION. This publication was occasioned by an apprehension, that some fanciful and dangerous
opinions were gaining ground among the multitude. The splendid
success of the French Revolution, the popular nature of its
principles, and the imperfect state of our representation, had
excited serious apprehensions that the affection of the people
would be alienated from the form of the government under which
we live. Struck with this apprehension, the writer of the first
Number submitted it to the inspection of a Friend,[3] who proposed, that it should be made the introductory paper of a series,
and recommended *Thoughts on the British Constitution*, as a title
that implied neither systematical composition nor methodical
arrangement. The papers were accordingly composed and published, in such order as the changes of the public mind or the
occurrences of the day required, and with such haste as the
occupations of the writers rendered indispensable. The order has
since been changed and some considerable additions made,
particularly in Numbers VII, XIII, XIV, XVI and XX. The suc-
cinct view exhibited in the ninth, tenth, and eleventh Numbers, of
the several plans which, at different periods, have been proposed
for a reform in the representation of the people in parliament, will
be prized as the first and only collection of the kind, by all sincere

friends of the measure. It was intended to subjoin the letters between PORTIA AND MR JONES, as calculated to throw light on a curious circumstance in history; but from the present size of the volume, they are necessarily omitted.[4]

Notwithstanding the number of these sheets, it is to be apprehended that no party has been convinced; and that any apparent change in the temper of the town has been occasioned by circumstances very different from dispassionate reflection, or conclusive argument.

The few who uniformly incline to the court, were for a considerable time compelled to give way to the popular torrent. They either maintained a prudent silence, or concurred with that party whose views appeared to be most moderate. Of late they have been more at liberty to avow their former opinions, being supported by the presence of a military force, and encouraged by the visible promptitude of the army.

The party who were lately predominant {the radicals}, and exerted their influence with that degree of moderation and decorum, which is to be expected from a triumphant faction, plume themselves on having been materially instrumental in effecting a change of popular opinions and political measures, in behalf of the Roman Catholics. They are persuaded, that this was occasioned by the Societies of United Irish-men in Belfast and Dublin, without whose alliance the Roman Catholics would have been treated in the manner recommended by the corporation of the metropolis, and the Grand Juries of the Kingdom. [5]

In answer to the objections which have been made to the nature and proceedings of these associations, they {the radicals} maintain, that in a country where the voice of the people is often disregarded, public opinion seldom consulted, and every thing carried either by the strong hand of power, or by the silent influence of the court, no signal advantage can possibly be obtained by ordinary means:–

That this circumstance warranted the extraordinary measure of establishing CLUBS, which formed a chain of correspondence, concentrated the popular strength, and demonstrated the possibility of bringing it into action:– That the violence of the means, was vindicated by the importance of the end; and the wisdom of the plan, evinced by its success. What has been accomplished[6] they look upon as a considerable step, not only to the entire emancipation of the Roman Catholics from every remaining restriction, but to a radical reform in parliament; for such, say they, must be the consequence of that permanent cordiality, which they suspect will subsist between the allied powers, and that spirit of liberty which they confidently look for among the great body of their new friends. The Catholics will labour inefficiently to effect a further renovation of the constitution; as all they have attained can be of little avail, while the boroughs which return two thirds of the commons, are the exclusive monopoly of the aristocracy in both houses. Their own interest therefore will secure their co-operation, and success will be certain.[7] They allege that the almost instantaneous change that took place in the minds of protestants, from intolerance to amity, proved the wisdom of the measures pursued, and the folly of that shallow system of enfranchisement, from time to time, which the opposing party so zealously contended for. – Acting on the most enlarged principle, and directed by the eternal rule of right, they would have blushed to demand liberty for themselves, while they denied it to others. Had they condescended to the weakness and fears of some of their townsmen, or followed the advice of timid friends, emancipation would never have come round; and the true advocates of the measure had no alternative, but to carry it by a sort of *Coup de Main*, as they did, or to lose both it and the reform, for ever. The success of the violent measures lately adopted by government,[8] they ascribe to the supineness of the nation the timidity of some, the bigotry of others, and the prevalence of aristocratic ideas in the higher orders of society. For their part, let the consequence be what it will, they scorn to make any compromise with bigotry and injustice; or to subject the Rights of Man to any temporizing modification.

Those {moderates}, who attempted in vain during the period treated of in this volume, to stem the tide of popular precipitation, are equally tenacious of their ancient notions; and as little disposed as formerly, to approve of the proceedings which they opposed. They draw a gloomy picture of the state of public affairs, and part-icularly of the condition of this town. They represent the country as having been reduced to servitude. They describe the place of their nativity as having been subjected to martial law; the emporium of commerce, become a military station; the inhabitants insulted and put to the sword in the streets, and the whole kingdom looking on with acquiescence: and then they exclaim. – Do our demagogues ever ask themselves how it came to pass that they were so deserted by their countrymen? that a land which for ten years past has been unanimously anxious for liberty, and particularly for a parlia-mentary reform, should muster but five counties at Dungannon, and that these counties should be viewed with suspicion by the rest of the kingdom;[9] that parliament should be unanimous, or nearly so, in passing the gunpowder and delegation acts, in suppressing the volunteers, in approving of the proceedings of the Lord's committees, such as private interrogatories, discretionary imprison-ment, and unlimited fines imposed by an extra-judicial sentence? Do they ever enquire how government could venture of such mea-sures at the eve of a war, and continue them after its commencement?

They {the moderates} insist that this cannot be owing solely to a daring or arbitrary spirit in government, to venality in parlia-ment, nor yet to an artful management of popular prejudice; BECAUSE government is the same, parliament the same, and the people the same. Nay, it is our boast that our people are better, more enlightened, more united, and more liberal. How then, they say, does all this happen?

They themselves, charge it upon three principles.

The FIRST is an affectation of secrecy and mystery, with a design of producing alarm; which, pervaded the measures of the United Irishmen, and afterwards infected the whole party. They contend that secret cabals are unconstitutional and unmanly, unfit for a free country or for free men; that no wise and good citizen will countenance societies whose members are unknown, whose pro-ceedings are secret, or whose designs and principles are concealed; that bad citizens will always endeavour to render them objects of jealousy; and that from this jealousy government will gain invin-cible strength. Tho' in some subjects obscurity may be a source of the sublime, in politics it is only a source of jealousy and distrust.[10]

The SECOND is an imitation of republican principles and language, accompanied with extravagant demands and menaces, published with a view to intimidation. This conduct alarmed all men of title, rank, and hereditary fortune, dissolved the opposition in parliament, prompted timid men to cling about the castle, or wish for a union with Britain; and inclined even some resolute and determined patriots to postpone a reform to calmer times.[11] An attempt to intimidate, when not founded on power, they assert is equally mean and ineffectual. It is dishonourable in a gentleman to bluster when he can do nothing, to say more than he means, and to use threats which he is neither able nor willing to execute; and it is ineffectual in a multitude to endeavour to outwit their governnors. They should employ nothing but plain and public declarations, or active force. If the people be unanimous, this will succeed; if not, it is vain for clubs and juntos to think of inspiring government with any permanent alarm. They may occasion a temporary dismay, till their weakness is discovered; but the artifice will soon be detected. Government have a multitude of agents, both voluntary and mercenary, in every district, who can soon ascertain the strength of a party; but the inhabitants of a country, scattered as they are over the whole face of it, have no such means of information. Government therefore will soon recover from their surprise, and industriously avail themselves of the occasion, by diffusing a distrust and disunion among the people, that one of their parties may join their standard. They will promote dissention among the subjects, to encrease the influence of the crown. Thus on the present occasion, the wily minister of our sister country[12] encouraged the Catholics when they were weak – then doubted of his ability to *perform* what he had given them reason to expect – advised them to apply to their own parliament – resisted their pretensions there – and at length brought all parties to depend upon Royal favour, as the only source of relief from domestic oppression. In this manner he carried off the glory of the measure, and insidiously endeavoured to attach the Catholics to the throne; dictated to parliament, and rendered the Cabinet of Saint James's a Court of appeal paramount to the legislature of Ireland. – This, (say they), is the present situation of affairs. Two knots of men in Dublin and Belfast, have disgusted and frightened the only persons who could in any case obtain a reform in the ways of peace.[13] They threw down the gauntlet. Government took it up. By their threatening language and warlike preparations, they seemed to say that they were able to obtain their demands by force. Administration knowing their imbecility, and feeling the additional strength it had acquired from such premature proceedings, said 'Let us try. – There is a proclamation for you; insulting, and you will say, unconstitutional. Is that enough?' All is quiet.– 'Here is a gunpowder bill. Won't that provoke you?' 'No.' 'We'll take your artillery. You sha'n't assemble in arms: and the people who shall disperse your darling volunteers are the police, the odious police.[14] Will nothing rouse you to put forth your boasted strength?' Even dragooning and military riots, in one part of this kingdom, were succeeded only by silent stupor and inaction.

The THIRD error, was separating Catholic emancipation from general reform. Under this head, they loudly declare, that they were as hearty in the cause of liberality as their opponents. They were as well disposed to unite Irishmen; but they knew that Protestant prejudices must be conciliated, as well as Catholic.[15] They wished for Catholic emancipation, but would have linked it with a system of general liberty. They wished to lead the people, in one phalanx, to demand a reform; and think that their force would then have been irresistible. As far as the feelings of Catholics are concerned, they rejoice in the extension of franchise; but as a national measure, their enfranchisement *without* a reform will be a calamity. – It will drown the few good voters we can boast of, in a deluge of the meanest class of Catholic electors. WITH A REFORM, this extension of franchise would have benefited ALL parties. They should therefore have gone hand in hand. Had this been the case, the Catholics would have remained with the people. They will now, it is apprehended, strengthen the hands of government, encrease the expense and corruption of elections, and render many of the old patriots tenacious of the boroughs, as a bulwark of the Protestant interest. They insist that the Protestant and Catholic should have been bound together by the tie of a common interest, a partnership in oppression, and a joint hope of freedom, which neither could obtain without the other.[16] This, they admit, would have required time; but that they do not think a material objection. Being apprehensive of sudden shocks in the political machine, they profess themselves friends to gradual and deliberate measures. Incredulous with respect to sudden revolutions in popular or religious prejudices, they fear that the progress of liberality, or decay of bigotry, is not by any means as great or general as is pretended; and that whatever views wise and enlightened men may take of the subject, three millions of people will not be easily excited to an opposition which some may consider dangerous to themselves, and others ungrateful to the court. A religious sect, whose dearest prejudices are in favor of Monarchy and Hierarchy, will scarcely prefer a combination either with associations suspected of republicanism, or with professed presbyterians, to an alliance with the State, and with the Church of Ireland, which they may consider as a sect of popery; since it acknowledges a human head, and professes to derive the efficacy of all its orders and ordinances, by apostolical succession thro' the Church of Rome.[17]

These they {the moderates} assert to have been their ideas; but finding the union of the clubs and the populace to be irresistible, and the advice and assistance of age, experience, approved integrity, and acknowledged abilities, rejected with disrespect, and being at the same time unwilling to obstruct so liberal a design, how much soever they deplored the mode of prosecuting it, – they very early withdrew their opposition; and thus precluded the dominant party from saying, that their plans had been thwarted, or their projects marred.[18]

The present paralytic state of the nation, (they say) is, by no means, the least pernicious consequence of these violent and premature exertions: nor is it the least extraordinary of those symptoms, which indicate this malady, that two county elections in which Belfast had always acted an honourable part, should pass unnoticed: that with respect to the County of Down in particular, a member should be returned without a poll, while the inhabitants of Belfast were first certainly informed of the name of the candidate by his advertisement of thanks.[19] The moderate party seem satisfied to submit to any imposition, rather than with a renewal of old disputes, and give an opportunity to popular agitators to disseminate their principles. The more decided patriots not only talk of elections as matters of no importance in the present state of things, but even express a wish, that grievances may encrease, that they may be the sooner and more effectually redressed. – Against this sentiment I most earnestly protest. It is the part of a good patriot, never to despair of the country, but in every situation to act for the best; and he must be a bad citizen or a shallow observer, who wishes that our political lethargy should encrease with the hope of being roused by a French reform. Such a man admits no medium between slavery, and revolution; the loss of liberty, and the subversion of all government. Amid ten thousand chances of despotism and anarchy, there is scarcely one of rational freedom; and this after a series of atrocious sanctions. – While these parties argue thus, the partizans of the castle[20] manage elections, as well as all other public business, at discretion.

Such are the views taken by both parties. It has been thought best to give them in the strongest language used by the partizan on either side, that the reader may perceive the force of their respective arguments, and be able to form an impartial judgement.

We cannot here forbear to remark, that the censure so lavishly heaped on the town which gave rise to this publication – is indefensible. Granting that a majority of those inhabitants who of late attended public meetings, were considered by the government of the country as having proceeded unwarrantable lengths – *twenty thousand* people are not therefore to be indiscriminately condemned. Of this we have sufficient proof, in the protest of two hundred and fifty five persons.[21] Among them were enrolled by far the greater number of those whose patriotism, moderation, and decision, had long given dignity and consistency to the proceedings of Belfast. Under such circumstances, what plea in wisdom could be found, for pouring in bodies of troops out of all proportion to the magnitude of the town, and consequently so scattered over it as to be beyond controul. What necessity demanded an union of the functions of a General with those of the Civil Magistrate;

removing an useful barrier between the ardour natural to the standing army, and the cool deliberation requisite in the execution of the law? In vain shall we search for an extenuation of the scenes of lawless violence which have so repeatedly occurred; or an excuse for exhibiting to the world a picture of the majesty of the laws prostrated. – THE LAWS, nothing should be suffered to trample upon with impunity, because their efficiency depends on public opinion; and the popular idea of their being omnipotent, is necessary to their support.

The civil power that should be superior on every occasion, seemed to sink under the exertion; and our streets displayed the occasional anarchy of Paris in miniature. Common sense informs us, that troops to make a figure in the field abroad, must practice subordination at home: and history says that the Pretorian bands of Rome, hastened the downfall of the Empire, and tyrannized over the very people that employed them.[22]

Belfast, by its consequence in the scale of Commerce, Manufactures, and Revenue, contributes eminently to the prosperity of the kingdom. It has paid near the rate of one hundred and twenty thousand a year in port duties alone, besides the incalculable share it otherwise takes in the general burthens of the state; and it has been said to have had a greater number of ships employed in *foreign* trade than all the rest of Ireland beside. Manufacturers experience in it the fostering hand of the most assiduous culture. When credit was tottering to its base in almost every corner of Europe, here it held its ground. Its merchants blended prudence with enterprize, and reaped the reward of unsullied integrity. In acts of munificence, in charitable institutions, and private donations, none will deny its merit. During the period of near a century and a half, from the usurpation of Cromwell, it was signalized as much for loyalty to its Prince and attachment to his government, as by zeal in the pursuit of civil liberty.[23] When our governors within these sixteen years dreaded a French invasion, and the Lord Lieutenant's secretary informed us, that government could only spare to the rich northern coast, the nominal protection of 'a troop or two of horse, or *part* of a *company* of *invalids*,' Belfast pressed forward in defence of the country. It was seen in arms, from the earliest dawn of that auspicious era, which opened with the enlargement of our trade, and closed with an acknowledgement of our national independence.[24]

With what precious care such a character should be preserved, and what lenity and protection those who possess it have a right to expect – need no illustration. Persecution in politics, as well as religion, is absurd. It rivets error, while it vainly attempts to check the progress of truth: But a mild administration of government disarms the violent, and confirms the zeal and influence of its friends. When we imagine we are forging fetters for human thought, we open new regions to its flight, enlarge the sphere of its action, and excite energies that were latent before.

*   *   *

We venture to pronounce, that valuable maxims in politics are to be drawn from the whole of these proceedings. They shew that there is danger of promoting general disaffection to the form of our government, if those who administer it practice a system of profligate expence, break thro' the best mounds of the constitution, and oppose every attempt at moderate reform. The alarm occasioned by the late exertions of a single town, and by the spirit which was diffusing itself over a respectable province, may satisfy rulers that tranquillity cannot be relied on, unless the will of the people be regarded, their complaints attended to, and their affections preserved. That the town which led the van, advanced too far beyond the main body, is sufficiently obvious. To that circumstance perhaps it is owing, that it failed in effecting still more important changes in national measures. But here, Ministers had little reason to boast. The people have a fund of unredressed grievances to reflect upon, and a spirit of discontent is consequently fostered in the most temperate bosoms. This may not always confine itself to the Northern Counties, but ultimately infect the thirty two.

Administration may then, have a chance of maintaining its authority, by the insidious policy of *dividing* the popular force: but how much more easily and more honorably might the same effect be produced, by *uniting* it? The worst governments should for their own safety rectify abuses that may in time undermine them, as a good one will encourage the natural tendencies of the constitution to renovate itself. The errors of France, as a beacon, point out the danger of *universal suffrage*; but instead of deterring government from a rational improvement in the representative branch of our legislature, they should stimulate them to grant, and the subjects to expect it. Had the Ministers of France made their appeal to the people in an earlier stage of the Monarchy, while the public mind was firmly attached, as ours is, to the Prince and to the form of his government, temperate measures would probably have been the result. That crisis was suffered to escape, and the consequences are to be deplored by every friend of liberty and order, in their own country and in the world.

On the whole, it were to be wished that from these petty broils, both government and its subjects would learn to guard against more lamentable convulsions, by attending to the following advice of MACCHIAVEL.

Let administration and the legislature study to render themselves so much beloved and respected by the people, that no party shall indulge a hope of disturbing them with success, or impunity: and let not a discontented faction be too confident, that the multitude, however disaffected, will support them in their enterprizes, or accompany them in their dangers.

Imparino pertanto i principi a vivere in maniera, e farsi in modo riverire e amare, che niuno speri potere ammazzandoli salvarsi; e gli altri conoschino quanto quel pensiero sia vano che ci faccia confidare troppo che una moltitudine, ancora che malcontenta ne' pericoli tuoi ti seguisti o ti accompagni.

STORIE FIORENTINE, lib. 7.[25]

CONTENTS OF THE VOLUME

Thoughts on the British Constitution

nation in that point. Charles Fox's advice to Ministers in hours of agitation.   77

Thoughts on the British Constitution

I feel a secret pride in thinking that I was born a Briton; when I consider that the ROMANS, those masters of the world, maintained their liberty little more than seven centuries; and that BRITAIN, which was a free nation above seventeen hundred years ago, is so at this hour.

OLDCASTLE[29]

TO

JAMES EARL OF CHARLEMONT,

THE ASSERTOR

OF THE

RIGHTS OF IRELAND,

AND

GENERAL OF ITS VOLUNTEER ARMY,

A FRIEND OF THE JUST PREROGATIVES OF THE CROWN,

AN ORNAMENT OF THE PEERAGE,

AND

PATRON OF A PARLIAMENTARY REFORM,

THESE ESSAYS ARE INSCRIBED;

WITH THE

DIFFIDENCE SUITED TO THEIR IMPERFECTIONS,

AND THE

RESPECT DUE TO HIS LORDSHIP'S VIRTUES,

AND

LITERARY ATTAINMENTS.[27]

Thoughts on the British Constitution
No. I[28]

The British Government is the only one in the annals of mankind that has aimed at the diffusion of Liberty through a multitude of People, spread over a wide extent of territory.

MILLAR'S HISTORICAL VIEW[29]

Thus was the present Constitution of our Government forming itself, for about two centuries and an half; a rough building raised out of the demolitions which the Normans had made, and upon the solid foundations laid by the Saxons. The whole fabric was cemented by the blood of our fathers; for the British Liberties are not the grant of Princes. They are original rights, conditions of original contracts, coequal with prerogative, and coæval with our Government.

OLDCASTLE

Belfast, 6 December 1792

At a period when REPUBLICS are exhibited as models of perfection, I am persuaded it is consistent with the spirit of a free press, to recommend the principles of the BRITISH CONSTITUTION. Though I reprobate whatever is unsound in our representation, which is too much the offspring of depopulated and corrupt boroughs, I am equally averse to unmixed democracy, for a country rooted in its love of unlimited monarchy. If the first is the origin of extravagance and rapacity, it admits of a cure: while the latter excels rather in speculation than practice, and points to scenes of confusion from which a good mind turns with horror.

With a fair representation of the people in Parliament, there would not I conceive be a Constitution on the earth comparable to the British: Let its theory be realized, and we shall seek in vain for another of such intrinsic excellence.

In contrasting it with the creations of yesterday, we must recollect that the seeds of decay are laid in every production, whether of nature or of art; that the most captivating forms of Government are not exempted from the common lot; and that the great searcher, time, alone can try their virtues or defects. In the vegetable world however, we find that the slower growths give the most solid timber; so in forms of civil polity, those which are the forced productions of a day, are neither best calculated for present use nor lasting existence.

It would be an easy task to trace the downfal of tyranny in FRANCE, to an emulation of British liberty among our Gallic neighbours. The admiration in which the essence of our Constitution was held by MONTESQUIEU, VOLTAIRE and ROUSSEAU, operated in fostering the love of liberty and undermining the false principles of the old monarchy.

With such innate vigour is this Constitution endued, that in spite of its corruptions it preserved the trial by jury many centuries after it was lost to other countries; and at this day secures the freedom of the press in a degree unknown in any former period.

AMERICA did not acquire her love of liberty in the new world, but carried it out from the old. – In forming a Constitution for herself, she retained several of the finest branches of the British, lopping off with a careful hand what she deemed excressences that had formed round the parent stem. The first appointment of a Sovereign, even a Washington, to a throne, would at his decease prove the source of jealousies without end: but she wisely created a Senate, and its good effects have been fully experienced. All the noble provisions of the common law of England, which it was the study of a certain great Civilian[30] to the latest period of his life to counteract, have been received into the American code, as means of promoting freedom and prosperity.

FRANCE either had a perfidious monarch, or one who did not rely on the people he pretended to trust:– Monarchy was therefore abandoned in that country.

If the power of the crown or of the Lords has encreased and should be diminished – RESTORE THE BALANCE. But let nothing ever tempt the good people of these realms even to imagine of a fabric which with all its errors has, time immemorial, been the veneration of the politician and philosopher – the boast of the countries that enjoyed it, and the envy of those that did not.

It is the fashion of the hour, and as ridiculous as most fashions are, to depreciate the Revolution of 1688 – and to despise the securities for our liberty, which that great transaction afforded. That Revolution expelled a Prince from the throne for attempting to govern without law. It preserved a spirit of freedom in these countries, which burst out again in America near ninety years afterwards; and travelling back, communicated its flame to Gallic slaves, converted in these latter days into free men, and become the hope of the world.

It is the fashion of the hour, to defend the wild position, that THE ENGLISH HAVE NO CONSTITUTION; and to apply indiscriminately to Kings, such indecent epithets as we should blush to use against the lowest of our species.[31] – If constitutions can only have existence on *parchment*, much of what is called the British is indeed but a name – for its foundation is the *unwritten* law of the land. If there never was a British one, for what purpose assembled the Barons at Runnymede?[32] – Why was Richard solemnly deposed by the suffrages of both houses, and the crown conferred on the

Duke of Hereford?[33] For what did *Hampden, Sydney* and *Russel*, sacrifice their lives?[34] – When *Charles* was brought to the scaffold, and the crown of *James* was torn from his brow, were not the actors in these scenes vindicating a constitution against the encroachment of princes, who had found that we possessed one, and wished to deprive us of it? – Is the united wisdom of ages, in which men of the first political eminence flourished, to be despised and rejected? – If ingenious arguments, raised latterly against the very ground-work of the British Constitution, and drawn merely from *its abuses*, be solid and convincing, every writer on the general principles of government, is a shallow reasoner and blockhead. Are such terms applicable to *Locke, Montesquieu, Rousseau, Voltaire, De Llhome,*[35] and the endless train of authors whose works claim immortality? – Have the ardent friends of freedom, in our own time, among whom we number FLOOD, GRATTAN, *Price, Jebb,* and *Wyvill,*[36] lost all pretension to common sense; and must we fix the charge of ideotism on every provincial and national convention in Ireland, as well as on the numerous English and Scottish societies, instituted for the express purpose of reforming errors in a constitution that has no existence but in the eye of fancy?

The first French assembly drew a plan of government on parchment, and raised their structure on a sublime *declaration of rights*; but it was hardly formed till their successors, after vain struggles with its errors, were obliged to raze it from its very base. Such are the virtues of a parchment constitution! – The present spirited, and, I believe, virtuous convention, is now creating a substitute for it, and that *a Republic.** Tho' they have every wish of the writer of this essay, that the Revolution may end in a substantial practical government, many years will the present generation have slumbered in the dust, ere its claim to a permanent existence can be established. There is no other form more liable to abuse, nor more subject to rapid change, than the one which perhaps necessity has obliged them to adopt, and which reason should certainly teach us to shun.[37]

The advocates for human rights, as all should be, will be convinced that the highest effort of genius and intellect may fall short in such an attempt, when he recollects the failure of *Locke* himself in forming a constitution for a British colony, with the purest principles of his own immortal work as his guide.[38] – To such errors will the noblest minds and the most enlightened assemblies be subject; when *theory alone* directs their path.

There is an absurd veneration of ancient establishments, which borders on folly and superstition – there is also a hardy contempt of the experience of ages, an inordinate love of innovation, and a desire of *destroying* where we might *repair*, that amount to presumption, and lead to ruin. Whether two living characters, whose books furnish the conversation of the present day, have sat for these portraits – the reader must determine.[39]

---

*   The new constitution alluded to above, has also since been laid aside, and a third produced. This third one abandons a fundamental point in the former, that was cried up as a new discovery in Republics, to wit, electoral assemblies appointed by the collective body of the people, and placed between them and the national legislature, for the election of the latter. The very matter which they have deserted was praised both in that country and this, as an infallible corrective of all the inconveniences of democracy. These instances are sufficient proofs of the inferiority of theory to practice. {*On this note, the Errata in the original edition, made a clarification*: 'mention was made of a third constitution having been framed for France; but it is apprehended that it was only a modification of the second one, which had been prepared by Barrere, Brissot, Condorcet, Danton, Gensonne, Petion, Sieyes, Thomas Paine, and Vergniaud'.}

Thoughts on the British Constitution
No. II[40]

Dans les monarchies la politique fait faire les grandes choses, avec le moins de virtue qu'elle peut.

ESPRIT DES LOIX, III, 5[41]

To produce great political good, less virtue is required in a monarchy, than in any other form of government.

14 December 1792

When a people think of framing a NEW CONSTITUTION, they should not choose the purest in theory, but the best that they can execute. If they fix upon one that requires greater integrity, economy, sobriety, and public spirit, than they possess, they will not be able to carry it into execution; and as the best things, when corrupted, become the worst, their visionary scheme will end in something worse than that which they had it in their power to secure.

If a DEMOCRACY, (which is a form of government conducted by popular assemblies, or in which promiscuous assemblies of the people have great influence over the legislature and the executive power) be chosen, the execution of the plan will depend on the multitude, or those who direct the multitude. While they continue perfectly wise, temperate, and upright, they will neither propose nor ratify any laws, except those which conduce to the public good. But should they at any time be addicted to folly, idleness, or corruption, all is lost. As the whole management and liberty of the country will then depend upon an ignorant, licentious, idle and profligate populace, whoever shall gain an influence over them may become master of the state. A democracy will then terminate in a DICTATORSHIP or EMPIRE, as in Rome; or in the dominion of a foreign power, as in Athens.

Every people, which is not altogether ignorant of human nature and of itself, will suppose this to be a possible case. Those, who have any knowledge of History, will take it for granted, that it will be the lot of every nation, at some time or other: and they will see cause to suspect that corruption will gain ground most rapidly where men are in the exercise of power and consequently most liable to temptation, that is, in a democratical REPUBLIC.

As this will happen some time or other, a wise man in deliberating on a new Constitution, will look for one, that will either answer a people, already corrupted; or that will execute itself, after they shall become corrupted. Otherwise they will be governed, only, while they require little or no government, which is the case of the Americans at present. A Constitution, formed on this plan, must consist of several branches, and must provide several checks.

Such is THE BRITISH CONSTITUTION. The KING, with a responsible council, presides in the executive department, and has a negative upon all laws proposed by the Lords or Commons; but cannot himself propose any. He has a great interest in the honour and prosperity of the state; but as he is liable to temptation, invested with great power, and may not always be sensible that his real dignity and happiness consist in the freedom of his subjects, he is by the practice of the Constitution forbid to act without his council; who are subject to be tried and punished either by impeachment or attainder. Lest this should not be a sufficient restraint, the Peers have individually a right of counselling the King: and the supplies depend upon the Commons.

Thus it agrees with the description of the Roman Constitution, under the Kings, as given by Sallust.[42] Imperium legitimum, nomen imperii regium habebant. – *Transl.* A government of law, tho' styled a monarchy.

The Lords act in two capacities, as the Supreme Court of Judicature, and as a Legislative Assembly. As a criminal court, they take cognisance of crimes against the state: as a court of civil appeal, they decide, in the last resort on cases of property: and as a branch of the legislature, they have a negative upon all laws; and a right of originating and amending all bills, except those which impose taxes. They are the heads of great and numerous families, and the proprietors of extensive landed estates; they are men destined from their birth to the exercise of these high functions; and it is reasonably expected that they should be educated so as to discharge them with ability. Some of them are men, who have risen from an inferior situation, by their abilities in public business, and their knowledge of the law. From all these considerations, there arises a probability that though they may often be misled by vanity, ambition, and partiality to the fountain of their honours, they will never concur in rendering the King *absolute*; nor in promoting any measure that may diminish the influence and dignity of their house, or strike at the prosperity of the kingdom, in which they and their numerous relatives and connections are so nearly concerned: because such innovations would at the same time destroy their own consequence.

The same hopes may be formed of THE COMMONS, who are elected for a limited term of years. The number of electors has varied at different periods, and is certainly at present too small.

Many of the members of the House of Commons, are, like the Lords, persons of large property, bound by personal interest to preserve the freedom and forward the improvement of the country; deeply interested in the good opinion of their fellow-citizens, and subject to rejection at the expiration of their trust. They have entire direction of the public treasure, are the Grand Jury of the nation in all state trials, and are competent by their power over the public purse to control the upper House and the King. It is however greatly to be lamented that they are frequently corrupted by influence and bribery: and it is yet more to be regretted that their constituents are too often liable to the same charge.

These constituents, with their fellow-citizens, form an additional check, a sort of FOURTH ESTATE; for the opinion of the people of England has been found capable more than once, of controuling every branch of the government, in its turn.

These are the principal wheels in this complicated machine. The theory, the practice, and the very principle of counter-action on which it is constructed, have all been made the subject of ridicule; and I have sometimes joined in the laugh; for I know that the wisest plans are often liable to the most ludicrous misrepresentations. But I have at a more serious moment derived solid satisfaction from reflecting, that it has been the instrument of establishing and securing, for a longer time than any other constitution, a greater degree of national liberty, prosperity, civilization, and knowledge, than was ever enjoyed by any other people, under any other form of government whatsoever.

The particular instances of the truth of this observation cannot be all enumerated in these limits. I shall therefore conclude for the present as I began, by mentioning one consequence of this order of things, which must appear of infinite importance to every one who has a due sense of the strong tendency to corruption, so visible in every community and every individual, especially when invested with power.

The point I allude to is this – No other form of government has ever been able to preserve the liberty and prosperity of the people in so depraved a state of society. Republican constitutions have answered well, while the people were able to govern themselves; but as fast as they began to require government, with the same haste did the constitution become incapable of affording it. The reason is plain; the people themselves were the administration, or the immediate directors of the administration; and they became frivolous, luxurious, extravagant and idle. If they had the framing of laws, they enacted, that the revenue appropriated to the maintenance of the navy should be applied to the support of the theatre, and made it a capital crime to *move* for the repeal of this law! – This was done by the Athenians, the most enlightened and patriotic people of antiquity. If they have only the election of representation in their power, they sell their votes to the highest bidder, and spend their bribes in deploring the degeneracy of the times, and planning a Revolution that will give them the whole of the plunder, which they are now obliged to share with their deputies. This last is the state of England and Ireland at present. It is plain that in a democracy this must speedily produce anarchy, and terminate in the arbitrary power of an individual. – But what is the state of affairs under the British Constitution? – The people have continued in this state of depravity for a great number of years, exposing their votes, and every thing that depends on their votes, namely, their liberty, civil and religious; their property, real and personal; to open sale in every county-town, city and borough in the kingdom, and only lamenting that the septennial and octennial fairs do not more frequently return. Now, notwithstanding this profligacy, the people of England enjoy, at this day, a greater degree of rational freedom, internal prosperity, and foreign power, united, than perhaps any other state of ancient or modern times. Il ne faut pas beaucoup de probité pour qu'un Governement Monarchique, ou un Governement Despotique se maintiennent, ou se soutiennent. La force des loix dans l'an, le bras du Prince, toujours levé dans l'autre, reglent ou contiennent tout. Mais dans un etat

Populaire il faut un ressort de plus, qui est la vertú. ESPRIT DE
LOIX, III, 3. *Transl.* A MONARCHIAL or Despotic Government can
support itself without much integrity in the people. The power of
law in the one, the arm of the Prince in the other, regulate every
thing. But in a popular state there must be something else to resort
to, and that is, virtue.

This proceeds from the system of checks and counteraction
which I have described. The King may desire to extend his
prerogative: but the two Houses are jealous of their privileges and
are backed by the people. The Lords may be partial to the Crown,
and willing to encroach on the Commons: but self-interest will
prevent them from sacrificing their consequence in the state; and
they find the Commons not less tenacious of their rights than able
to maintain them. – The Commons are an over match for both the
Monarchial and the Aristocratical branches, and have nothing to
fear from their union: but should they abuse their power, in opposition to the sense of the nation, we have seen that their constituents
will defeat the ambitious projects of their own representatives: and
on all such occasions, the King can appeal to the people, by a
dissolution of Parliament.

Thus it has happened, that every branch of the Government
may be corrupt, and meditate unconstitutional encroachment on
the rest; nay the people themselves may be sunk in gross corruption,
and yet the country be free and prosperous. – This cannot be said
of any Government except *the British*.

Thoughts on the British Constitution
No. III[43]

The executive power ought to be in the hands of a MONARCH; because this branch of government is better administered by ONE than by MANY. – If there was no Monarch, and the Executive Power was committed to a certain number of persons, selected from the Legislative Body – THERE WOULD BE AN END THEN OF LIBERTY.

MONTESQUIEU[44]

18 December 1792

The page of history is stained with the crimes of Kings. They are charged not only with their own, but those which have been perpetrated in their names. Almost all Kings have been absolute monarchs; and their passions being thus released from controul, have run into the wildest excess. – But there is no doubt that they have often been made accountable for enormities in which they had no share. They have been loaded with obloquy on account of the effects of state policy, of the ambition of their subjects, of court fatigue, and personal resentment, of which they have been only the dupes. Every thing that happens during the reign of a King is imputed to himself; though he may have been an innocent as Edward VI when he signed the writ (de hæretico comburendo) for burning the anabaptist woman.[45]

Monarchy is falling into disrepute, because we have seldom had examples of Monarchs properly limited. Kings acquired their power, either by conquest, or feudal pre-eminence. The power conferred by conquest is unbounded: and the feudal chief considered his people as vassals. The royal houses of Europe are chiefly indebted for their crowns to the feudal system and the usages of the northern barbarians. According to the strength or weakness of the Barons, were the restrictions of the royal authority. For many generations the Barons, or Lords, were the only opposers of despotism; and England, in particular, is indebted to them for MAGNA CHARTA, and for confining the King within some moderate limits, until THE COMMONS became of sufficient consequence to join in the opposition.

The influence of the Commons arose from the introduction of commerce, and from the privilege obtained by the Lords under Henry VII of alienating their lands, which the merchants were then able to purchase. This strengthened the opposition, and confirmed the limitation of the prerogative. In *France*, the downfall of the Barons was the exaltation of the Throne; in England, it contributed to its limitation, by strengthening the Commons.

Whether the King of England is even now sufficiently restricted, is a question which may come under consideration at another time – at present I mean only to offer some remarks in favour of LIMITED MONARCHY; and what I have premised may justify me in saying, that no conclusion can be drawn against this branch of our Constitution, from the personal vices of arbitrary tyrants, nor from the miseries occasioned by despotism. There is a greater distance between the absolute power of a despot, and the regulated authority of a King, who is considered as the president or chief magistrate of the state, than between the fury of a mob, and the wisdom of a well constituted Republic.

With respect to foreign affairs, it is, I believe, admitted by every respectable writer on politics, that a monarchy excels in three very important particulars – secrecy – vigour – and dispatch; and with regard to internal tranquility, it is attended with this invaluable advantage, that it extinguishes the hopes of turbulent ambition.

All the Republics of antiquity, except LACEDEMON,[46] were torn by incessant convulsions, through the intrigues, real or imaginary, of powerful citizens, aiming at the supreme authority. These occasioned more misery, than all the fictitious plots invented in other countries, by Kings or their ministers. Lacedemon escaped those plagues by combining a limited monarchy with a democratical government. The throne was considered as the indisputable hereditary property of two branches of the family of *Hercules*. The division of the royal authority between two co-existing Kings would seem to be an abundant source of discord and contention, yet the effect was, that the peace of the State was never disturbed by any pretenders to the throne.

Athens was so distracted by attempts to seize upon the supreme power, or by the fear of despotism, that she was obliged to resort to the extraordinary expedient of banishing, by ostracism, every citizens who excelled the rest in abilities, or even in the most harmless virtues. The Athenian who voted for the exile of *Aristides*, could give no other reason for his conduct than this – that he was grieved to hear him called Aristides *the just*.[47] This is a striking instance of a general truth, that envy is despot of Republics.

Rome was continually engaged in such struggles. Valerius, justly surnamed Poplicola, or the courtier of the populace, had scarcely expelled the *Tarquins*, when he was accused of a design to restore royalty in his own person.[48] Manlius fell under the same suspicion, and was thrown from the Tarpeian Rock, soon after he had, with his single arm, defended it against the Gauls.[49] The Decemvirs attempted to perpetuate their authority.[50] The Consuls and Senate were, almost every year, obliged to resign the lives and liberties of the people into the hands of a *Dictator*. The contests of *Marius* and

Sylla, *Cæsar* and *Pompey*, *Octavius* and *Anthony* – conducted the Republic through a series of calamities to her final extinction.[51]

Thus in Republics, the abilities of the greatest men are either extinguished by banishment, and transferred to the enemies of the state; or they become the pests of their country, by indulging an inordinate ambition. In the first instance, the country becomes subject to a foreign power, like *Philip of Macedon* – in the other, to a domestic tyrant, who having obtained a victory over the rights of his fellows, will never think himself safe, while a free, or a daring, or a virtuous man exists among his subjects. – Regibus boni, quam mali suspectioris sunt: semperque his aliena virtus formidolosa. – SALLUST BELL. CAT.[52] *Transl.* The good are always more suspected by despots than the bad: merit is ever formidable to them.

Such was the line of the Roman Emperors. A LIMITED MONARCHY avoids these extremes. The monarch has no rivals to fear, and of course has no incentive to cruelty. – The principal citizens have no hope of attaining the supreme authority, and must confine themselves to more innocent objects of ambition.

The greatest nobleman in England has no more chance of ascending the throne, than the meanest peasant. – In Republics, the ablest citizens waste and abuse their abilities in ambitious and ruinous projects: in absolute Monarchies, they conceal them altogether, or sacrifice them to the will of the Prince. But in a limited Monarchy, none can raise his hopes to the crown: none can rise to any true greatness, except by serving the state, and by the good opinion of his fellow subjects.

L'ambition est pernicieuse dans un Republique. Elle a de bon effets dans la Monarchie. – ESPR. DES LOIX. III. 7. *Transl.* In a Republic, ambition is pernicious; in a Monarchy beneficial.

The same arguments as well as the authority of history, recommended hereditary, in preference to elective Monarchy. An elective Monarchy threatens intestine wars; desperate conspiracies; cruel precautions; and bloody revenge. Upon this point I presume the public are nearly of one mind: since we all joined so heartily in applauding and supporting the abortive revolution of POLAND, in which the change from an elective to an hereditary Monarchy was a striking feature.[53]

How far the evils attendant on the *old Republics* may be obviated by the *Representative* form, may be considered hereafter.

Thoughts on the British Constitution
No. IV[54]

Point de Monarque, point de Noblesse; point de Noblesse; point de
Monarque, mais on a un despote.

ESPRIT DE LOIX, II. 4

No King, no Nobility; no Nobility, no King, but in his stead a despot.

SPIRIT OF LAWS, II. 4

25 December 1792

The histories of all governments give testimony to the superiority
of the principles of our own. To these it may probably be restored,
if the people have the spirit, virtue, and wisdom, to draw their force
to a point – to a reform of ACKNOWLEDGED ABUSES IN THE
REPRESENTATION.

This language will not be understood by any who wish to
distract public attention, and draw it off to the Utopian schemes
with a distempered imagination. With such men, whatever is good
in our present frame of government, is to be involved in one
common wreck, with what is bad. Every speck on its surface,
becomes a mountain; and whatever is venerable and noble,
diminishes to a point.

Its ABUSES are great, but its good qualities are many. To remove
the one, and preserve the other, is the first aim of a patriot.

My last contained general remarks on the advantages peculiar to limited Monarchy; contrasted with the incessant convulsions incident to a *Republic*.

The HEREDITARY BRANCH of our legislature, now naturally rises into view.

In the endless Philipics, against the constitution, the House of Lords has been one of the principal butts of satire. – Many of its enemies are enemies of the whole system, as they would be of any other that chance had connected them with, and they attack at this point; conceiving it the weakest in the line. They are either those who will not perceive excellence in any thing short of absolute perfection; or who prefer a political storm to the blessing of liberty under a serene sky.

That several nobles have rendered themselves odious to the best friends of order in our country, we need not be surprised. A removal however of the cause of aversion, must in the sober eye of reason, claim a preference to the absolute extinction of an essential part of our government.

The nobles early laid one of the broadest foundations of our liberty in the reign of King John; and at different periods since that æra, they have preserved or restored the political balance.

Montesquieu, in exploring the private springs of the rise, declension, and fall of Empires, draws this striking picture; which is recommended as an original, to the young political connoisseur. – 'A very curious spectacle it was in the last century, to behold the impotent efforts the English made for the establishment of democracy. The government was continually changing. The people, amazed at so many revolutions, fought every where for a democracy – without being able to find it. At length after a series of *tumultuary motions and violent shocks*, they were obliged to have recourse to THE VERY GOVERNMENT which they had so odiously proscribed.'[55]

To return to the Lords: it is too true that many of them, in contempt of the constitution, in defiance of the spirit of the law and the votes of the Commons, have usurped an undue and almost ruinous dominion in the state, by monopolizing rotten insignificant BOROUGHS, and often returning representatives of themselves to the house of the people. To that cause, they owe all the odium in which several of them are held; and if they should ever cease to exist as a distinct order, to that source may they trace it. But it is in their individual capacity that we are to blame them; for in their legislative one, Lord Chatham[56] I think has told us, that their power comparatively with that of the Commons, is as a drop of water to the ocean.

Strip them of their constitutional influence over elections, and every solid objection vanishes. Were we to contemplate a House of Lords, divested of all influence in the return of the representative assembly, we should only see in it advantage and safety to the commonwealth.

The necessity for two deliberative powers, was thus asserted by *De Lolme*, who says – 'that the laws of a state may be *permanent*, it is necessary that the LEGISLATIVE POWER should be *divided*: That they may have *weight* and continue in force, it is necessary that THE EXECUTIVE POWER should be *one*'.[57]

It was well understood both by the GREEKS and ROMANS; for a senate made part of their most democratical constitutions, as the surest means of preventing precipitation and error. The senators, in some states, held their seats for life; and in many Roman families, the office even seems to have been hereditary.

In a monarchical government, it is indispensibly necessary; and on that point it has been well said, that there cannot be a greater solecism in politics than a nobility who suffer the liberty of the Commons to be taken away. In aristocracies the nobility get whatever the commons lose; but in monarchies, the crown alone is gainer; and the certain consequence of their helping to enslave the Commons, is their being enslaved themselves at last.

If we take the range of history under our eye, we shall see in the Lords a permanent body that survives when the representative branch perishes; and has more than once prevented the ruin of the constitution, when the monarch would have levelled its barriers.

Did a prince wish no longer to summon new parliaments, after the demise of an old one, we should experience in the Lords a body as imperishable as royalty itself; entitled by privilege to demand an audience with the despot; ready to advise a revival of the ancient forms; and urged by its own interest to oppose him by force if he refused it.

When the Commons House dissolves, the noble branch stands entire – and armed with the strength of the nation, has ere now vindicated its cause with their own. We naturally lose sight of its use, because it is most apparent, when the machine of state is most in peril; while by the natural operation of our government it loses its force, when all is tranquil and secure.

Neither the limited nature of this publication, nor the time of the writer, admit of more than rapid sketches; else might innumerable cases be stated in which the Lords would naturally stand in the breach, and where they actually have done so. I shall briefly mention four, at very different periods. 1. – We are indebted to them for the Great Charter of our Liberty, acquired so early as 1215. 2. – At a time when the Roman, or civil law, now the ecclesiastical law in these kingdoms, was an object of admiration over Europe, the Lords opposed its introduction into England, tho' it was recommended there with the utmost zeal, by the clergy. Had it not been for the determined part then taken by the Peers in favour of the common law, we should not at this day have it to boast of, but be governed by the Justinian Pandects,[58] in its stead. In the reign of Richard II the nobility in Parliament declared their disapprobation, in these pointed terms – 'The realm of England hath never been unto this hour, neither, by the consent of our Lord the King, and the Lords of Parliament, shall it ever be, ruled or governed by the civil law.'[59] Of course to their interference on that occasion we owe the broadest foundation of our liberties. 3. – On the dissolution of government by the flight of *James*, they saved the state from destruction, by instantly holding the reigns of empire for the people, issuing orders to the fleet, the army, and the garrisons, and corresponding with the Prince of Orange about the means of saving the nation. When the Convention–Parliament met, they cavilled not at the self appointment of the Commons, but acted boldly in conjunction with them, and a Revolution was effected that has had few parallels in history, either for the orderly manner in which it was conducted, or the ends it attained.[60] 4. – And, so lately as George the First, they passed a bill for limiting *their own* numbers; which, tho' a highly salutary restriction of regal prerogative, was lost in the lower house.

The advantages of a dernier court of appeal, of a court for trying charges of high crimes and misdemeanours, and for the impeachment of ministers – have seldom, if ever, been denied. A supreme judicial authority is therefore vested in the Peers, as men guarded against the influence of bribery and corruption, by numbers, permanent wealth, and hereditary name.

The necessity for a middle branch being proved by history and argument, it follows that it must have a *negative* vote; in order at once to afford a third or casting voice, to preserve a balance, and secure its own existence.

Respecting the spiritual Lords, little need be said. In their capacity as clergymen, they have no right to fit in Parliament; for it is merely as persons possessing baronies under the Crown, or by fiction supposed to do so, that either the Bishops of this day, or the Abbots of a former one, could rest any claims of seats among the

Lords. Their having them, serves neither religious nor civil liberty, and yet less the progress of a further reformation in the Church. Tho' some improvement might be made in this point, I perceive that as Spiritual Barons, they would not weigh a grain in the scale against A HOUSE OF COMMONS, really returned by *the People*.[61]

In favour of a divided legislative power, or middle estate, the annals of past ages from the earliest period to the highest cultivation of the human mind, bear evidence; and only yesterday it has been the free choice of *America*, which in the heat of war adopted it into its constitution. After a deliberate consideration in times of peace, they retain it both in their provincial and federative legislatures. The writer would not be surprised to find that even *France*, profiting by experience, should adopt it hereafter.

With the words of an author, whose book should survive the language it was written in, I will close this paper.

A body of nobility is also more peculiarly necessary in our mixed and compounded constitution, in order to support the right of both the crown and the people, by forming a barrier to withstand the encroachments of both. It creates and preserves that gradual scale of dignity, which proceeds from the peasant to the Prince; rising like a pyramid, from a broad foundation, and diminishing to a point as it rises. It is this ascending and contracting proportion that adds stability to any government; for when the departure is sudden from one extreme to another, we may pronounce that state to be precarious. – The nobility therefore are the pillars, which are reared from among the people, more immediately to support the throne; and if that falls, they must also be buried under its ruins.[62]

Thoughts on the British Constitution
No. V[63]

No temptation shall ever induce me to join any association that has for its object a change IN THE BASIS of our constitution, or an extension of any of these bases beyond the just proportion. It was not (thank God) made in a day. It is the result of gradual and progressive wisdom. It has grown up in a *series*; and never, never, has the guardian protecting genius of England been either *asleep* or *satisfied*.

> CHAS. FOX – Speech on the 13th Dec. 1792,
> against the proclamation[64]

1 January 1793

THE CONSTITUTION; the whole CONSTITUTION; and nothing but THE CONSTITUTION. – These few words comprehend the political creed of the author of this paper. – With the whole constitution, he is neither a friend of liberty, order, nor peace, who will not rest content. Without it, no man should.

The great body of the Commons of Ireland, would then have a full representation in their own House of Parliament – and the democracy be restored in its due weight in government.

The power over the purse of the nation, over the sinews of war, commerce, and manufactures, over every thing that gives influence among men, being thus returned to its rightful owners – corruption would be trampled under foot, as the means of corrupting

would be removed. The right of the people to originate laws, thro'
their representatives, and, to prevent improper ones by their *veto*,
would be at the same time effectually secured.

No longer should we hear of auctions, auctioneers, and pur-
chasers of the Peerage; of the vile traffic in boroughs; or of
ministerial profligacy and extravagance. AXES we should still
have; for without them, only savages in the hunting state can exist;
and if the feeling, rather than reflecting MILLION, ever think
otherwise, they are deceived. But these expences would be regulated by wisdom, and confined within those bounds which the
necessities of the commonwealth prescribe.

Such are the effects to be expected in the common course of
things, from a House of Commons, the express image of the
collective body. But to entitle it to this character, I do not hesitate
to assert, that the basis of election must be extended to ROMAN
CATHOLICS. They are *men*, with all the energies of our nature.
By the cultivation of their native powers and feelings, the stock
of national virtue, spirit, and freedom, may be encreased as well
as improved. I must remark in this place, that their ancient
prepossessions, and their recent declarations, are all in favour of
three estates; the defence of which, is one of the objects of these
brief essays.

We have lived to see systematic corruption not only practised in
secret, but *avowed* by administration. We have known charges of
the highest crimes against the Majesty of the state, against the
fountain of honours, and the unsullied purity that should distin-
guish the nobles of the land, ready to be made, but refused a hearing;
tho' the guardian of his country was the accuser, and millions of
wronged subjects were impatient for the issue. From such a scene
it is natural to turn away with disgust; and pointing at the deformed
figure, to acclaim, – *Is this our glorious and happy constitution?* But
let her appear in her native colours, and the attentive spectator will

discern the complexion of health, the lines of beauty, and the proportions of strength. Even in her present condition, we see the remains of a gigantic and venerable form, retaining such vigour in old age as few other constitutions exhibit in youth. Encrease the circulation by a new portion of the vital principle, and our government may long remain a blessing to all who enjoy it; an example of one of the finest theories of antiquity, realised. For such was the constitution which Polybius[65] described as the perfection of human contrivance, 500 years before the Saxons, HENGIST and HORSA, had landed on British ground;[66] and such was the Constitution which Cicero praises in the following words – 'Statuo esse optime constitutam rempublicam quæ ex tribus generibus illis regali, optimo, et populari confusa modice, nec puniendo irritet animum immanem et ferum, nec omnia prætermittendo licentia cives deteriores reddat.' – *Cic. Frag.* Lib. 2. de Rep. – I lay it down (he says) as a maxim, that that state is best constituted, which being composed of the three forms, royal, aristocratic, and popular, neither exasperates the unruly and ferocious mind of the multitude, by severity; nor corrupts the people, by licentious indulgence.[67]

What government is the most desirable, most congenial to the nature of human beings? – That which does not need an incessant and unrelaxed action of *the whole* people to keep it alive; but which, by frequent periodical calls, reminds them of the rights of man, and the constitution of their government. Not that which can only exist by continual appeals to *every* member of the community, which rests on the unremitting activity and heroic virtues of each, and tumbles into ruin when deprived of these precarious supports. Such an one is neither calculated to promote the most durable liberty, nor happiness of men.

In the first moments of popular ardour, where the sinews of every individual fight the battles of the country, the successes of a new people may dazzle others sunk in torpid repose; but they are by no means proofs of the future excellence or stability of their embrio constitution.

The great Author of Nature never but for the highest purposes of wisdom, suspends the laws of his government. Tracing an analogy between his works and those of his creatures, we may pronounce, that structures which are most hastily erected, have the worst chance of lasting existence; whilst those which spring from occasions, and grow out of the wants of the human soul – may be considered as resting on foundations laid by a divine hand.

Thoughts on the British Constitution
No. VI[68]

By the corruption of Parliaments, and the absolute influence of a King or his Minister on the two Houses, we return into that state, to deliver us, or secure us from which, Parliaments were instituted. Our whole constitution is at once dissolved. Many securities to liberty are provided; but the integrity which depends on the freedom and the independency of parliament, is the keystone which keeps the whole together. If this be shaken, our constitution totters; if it be quite removed, our constitution falls into ruin. That noble fabric, the pride of Britain, the envy of her neighbours, raised by the labour of so many centuries, repaired at the expense of so many millions, and cemented by such a profusion of *blood*; that noble fabric, I say, which was able to resist the united efforts of so many races of GIANTS, may be demolished by a race of PIGMIES.

BOLINGBROKE[69]

12 January 1793

It is now near two thousand years since Polybius, in contemplating the various defects to which governments were subject, conceived a mixture of the elements of each, that was to avoid the errors of all. He probably did not entertain a hope, that the bold flight of his fancy would be realized in the revolution of time; that the system would prove as excellent in practice as it was in theory; and that its pre-eminence would be placed beyond the possibility of doubt, by its having among its other virtues the valuable one of *stability*.

His speculation was founded on the nature of MAN; else that would at this day remain only the monument of a fine imagination, which our rude ancestors enjoyed long after in their native woods. – They enjoyed the spirit and essence of the British Constitution: and if we are asked in what records the charter of their liberties is to be found, we answer with HUME, that 'it was not writ on parchment, not yet on leaves, or barks of trees; for it preceded the use of writing and all other civilized arts of life.'[70]

It is one of the many perfections of that constitution which, with a necessary reform, these papers counted for, that it has the peculiar faculty of recovering after every fall; instead of gradual declension, and dissolution. Even the commanding mind of CROMWELL, could only change its monarchical outline for a season; and CHARLES and JAMES suspended the democracy in its composition, at the expence of the head of the one, and the crown of the other. The machine felt transient convulsions, but reverted back to its original state with more celerity than it had departed from it.

So deeply laid in the constitution is the spirit of liberty, that it rose superior to the power of the Plantagenets, Tudors, and Stuarts, and to every attack from every quarter.

To revive its spirit, we have only to recur to its first principles; and, clearing away the rubbish of centuries, erect the popular pillar of government on a foundation which shall at once procure security to the crown, stability to the peerage, and liberty to the people.

'The *fee-simple is in* US.' We can revise and amend, or rather restore; for the structure contains within itself materials for its repair.

Strengthened by the opinions and actions of the greatest men in modern times, without a single contrary authority, till within the two last years, – many contend, that the *constitution* is not merely a name, but A REALITY: – others allege, that to the latter character it has no pretensions, because it is not FIXED and WRITTEN – and because it *is* ALTERABLE by the King, Lords, and Commons. – But all agree, that a reform in the Commons House is an object in the highest degree desirable; and that by *unity* and *perseverance*, it may be effected.

Let every honest heart and hand, then, be applied to bring it about. In the disunion of the people, evil governors found their hopes; in an adherence to simple points, they have their greatest fears.

It little concerns me what party is either pleased or displeased by the freedom of these THOUGHTS, as they are dictated by a genuine affection for my native land; by an aversion to every power that would trample on the rights of my fellow men; and by a sincere sorrow for all their wanderings from the plain line of practicable good. My regard for a radical reform is sufficiently evinced; as my object is to promote an union among the people of Ireland, and to urge those under whose eye these papers may fall, to direct their hopes to ONE undisputed point. In that point ALL meet; and against the necessity of attaining it, the most corrupt courtier, pensioner, or sycophant, no longer presumes to offer an argument.

With those virtuous men, whose sole object is a fair organ through which the will of the people may be declared in Parliament, I trust, that the one grand object may be pursued with steady decision; and that spirit and moderation may be so happily co-mingled, that on the heads of Governors shall fall any evil that can follow. Every thing bordering on precipitation or intemperance, would be ruin and defeat. If the nation, as an aggregate whole, come fairly and decidedly forward – success will follow. But even the thoughtless agitator should beware how matters are pushed to extremes, ere the counties and the provinces are ready to speak and to act. Such men are apt to look from the spot they inhabit, as the soul of a system; to imagine that its rays illume the farthest verge of the circle; and that the same ardent heat prevails at the extremities which is felt at the center.

To *those invested with power*, I beg leave to address a few words. They should hear them with the greater candour, as they come from one who detests levelling and republican principles, as much as he condemns the blemishes that deface our Constitution. To restore the weight properly belonging to each of the three powers, is the utmost extent of his wish; and that wish has not only reason, but millions to support it.

From an attentive observation of the growth of public opinion, of what has passed and is passing in the minds of men, I aver that the feint approbation of the measure, which formerly convoked county meetings, and provincial ones, a volunteer convention, and a civil assembly of delegates, has at length given way to a desire of reform, which animates every breast, and whispers that the rights of the people, pursued even in the ways of peace, cannot long be withheld. That it is not now as it once was, confined to a virtuous few, who with unceasing labour fanned the spark – but actuates every honest man, of every rank. It is not restricted to the needy, to whom scenes of confusion afford profit and delight; but embraces all, or almost all, the gentlemen of landed property in *Ulster*, not within the baleful influence of a Court. They join in the general prayer for a reform, as public tranquility and the WILL OF THE NATION require it. They are those who have most to contend for, and to whom peace and the security of property must ever be dear; but their judgment concurs with that of every thinking man, that a gracious and well timed concession may ensure the loyalty and happiness of Ireland for generations. A wise statesman would even in times of profound peace investigate this great canker in the state; nor in war should he shrink from it.

This is the interest of the King, and the King's friends; of the People, and the People's friends – may it be considered with the seriousness which the subject deserves!

Procrastination is dangerous; decision, wisdom. There are times when moderate improvement would be accepted with pleasure and content, that at a more advanced stage would be rejected with scorn. Let no man pretend that principles unfriendly to the spirit of the Constitution, are widely disseminated – if there are such, they lurk in a few breasts, and are too feeble to infect the general mass. Every society of Citizens, every Volunteer body, every Catholic meeting, disclaims them – and rests their hopes singly on AMENDMENT, not SUBVERSION.

If government require a lesson, they may receive it from a Statesman, qualified to steer thro' a tempestuous ocean. With his advice, therefore, given in Parliament on the 13th ult. shall this number conclude.

CHARLES FOX'S ADVICE TO MINISTERS

What, it may be asked, would I propose to do in hours of agitation like the present? I will answer openly. If there is a tendency in *the Dissenters* to discontent, because they conceive themselves unjustly suspected and cruelly calumniated, what should I do? I would instantly repeal *the Test and Corporation Acts*, and take from thereby all cause of complaint. If there were any persons tinctured with a republican spirit, because they thought that the representative government was more perfect in a republic, I would endeavour to *amend the representation of the Commons*, and to prove that the House of Commons, though not chosen by ALL, should have no other interest than to prove itself *the representative of all*. If there were men dissatisfied in Scotland or Ireland, or elsewhere, on account of disabilities or exemptions, of unjust prejudices, and of cruel restrictions; I would repeal the penal statutes, which are a disgrace to our law book. If there were other complaints of grievance, I would redress them where they were really proved; but above all, I would constantly, cheerfully, patiently, LISTEN. I would make it known that if any man felt, or thought he felt a grievance, he might come freely to the bar of this House, and bring his proofs. And it should be made manifest to all the world, that where they *did exist*, they should be redressed; where they did not, that it should be made manifest. If I were to issue a proclamation, this should be my proclamation: 'If any man has a grievance, let him bring it to the bar of the Commons House of Parliament, with the firm persuasion of having it honestly investigated.' These are the subsidies that I would grant to Government. What, instead of this, is done? Suppress the complaint – check the circulation of knowledge – command that no man shall read; or that as no man under 100*l.* a year can kill a partridge, that no man under 20 or 30*l.* a year shall dare to read or to think.

Thoughts on the British Constitution
No. VII[71]

> The English Colonies in North America are entitled to certain rights, by the immutable laws of nature, the principles of the British Constitution, and the several CHARTERS or COMPACTS.
>
> [*Declaration of American Congress in* 1774]

12 February 1793

The word CONSTITUTION, has a variety of significations. In a general sense it means the act or manner in which any thing is constituted, or the parts of which it is composed. When applied to *politics*, it sometimes expresses the component or constituting members of a government; as when we say, that King, Lords, and Commons, are the constitution of Great Britain. At other times, it means certain principles, laid as a foundation, on which a future government may be built: but as it has seldom happened, that people had an opportunity of proceeding so methodically, this, 'till of late, was a very unusual sense of the word. – The signification, which it has obtained in England and Ireland, is a COLLECTION OF FUNDAMENTAL RIGHTS, which were early asserted and established by the people; to which by long habit and experience they have become firmly attached, and which they conceive to be essential to the continuance of their liberties.

If England has *no* constitution, there never was one in the world till within these seventeen years; and all the nations of antiquity as well as of modern times, were slaves. Whoever has been gulled by such a deceitful position, may blush for a shameful surrender of his understanding.

Let us for an instant, look to AMERICA; the only country in which it seems there *is* a constitution. What is her constitution, deservedly boasted, and well calculated as it is, for the manners of the inhabitants? It is a declaration in writing of most of the primary principles of that very British one, the existence of which is questioned! These principles HAVE existed and DO exist in force, after the revolution of many ages. America has not only found, but traced them, in legible characters. She has given them 'a visible form' and wisely adopted them into her system; as far as it was practicable, from the difference between the authority of a President, and that of a King.

He who searches with candour, will be at no loss to find the British Constitution in CHARTERS; in statute and common law; in immemorial MAXIMS AND PRACTICES; and in that unrivalled system of PRINCIPLES, from which these have issued. John Adams the Vice President of the United States, has within these two years informed us, that it lies in a venerable body of unwritten or customary laws, sanctioned by the accumulated experience of ages, and by statutes.[72]

We will briefly try how far this is founded. – The Constitution, at so early a period as the Saxons in England, establishes our right to a government by laws, framed by those who are to be governed; and to the trial by Jury. It establishes our right to very general suffrage; for from the reign of *Alfred* in 871, to the 7th of Henry IV* and from thence to 8th Henry VI in 1429,† every free male

---

*   7th Hen. IV enacts, that 'All those that there be present, as well sureties duly summoned for this cause, as others, shall attend to the election of *their* Knights for the Parliament; and then, in full county, shall proceed to election freely and *indifferently*, notwithstanding any request or commandment to the contrary.'

inhabitant was, or might be, an elector. During Henry's minority (when he was crowned King of France at Paris) a law was enacted confining elective franchize to persons possessed of a freehold worth 40s. per annum.

It establishes our right to very frequent elections of Parliament: for they were held twice in every year down to 1400. The good old custom of frequent Parliaments, was declared by statute 4.

I am far from adducing this instance of an early *statute*, respecting universal suffrage in counties, as an argument for its adoption in the present altered circumstances of society. It is one of those points, on which the best friends of reform may hold dissimilar opinions; on which nothing should tempt us to split. Certainly, general liberty may be well maintained, without the communication of franchise to paupers, vagabonds, and the lowest order of the state. It can never be denied that the strict line of theoretical right goes the full length, but we are obliged to desert that, when we exclude every male that happens to be a single hour short of twenty-one years of age; as well as those who cease to be minors, between the termination of one election and the commencement of another. If we must thus, in order to produce the greatest good, exclude a monstrous proportion of all the male inhabitants of a country, on the score of mental incapacity during non-age; on the same principle, persons dependant on others, through poverty or servitude, are as ill qualified to perform the duty of free agents as the youth of eighteen, nineteen, or twenty. And we need not be informed that these periods are the most favourable to virtuous enthusiasm, as well as least liable to selfish passions. Beside these arguments, it may be alleged that COMMERCE, that great spring of political independence, as well as the fixed interest in LAND, should be protected by parliamentary representation. I shall add another consideration, which has engaged the attention of the writers on this subject. Our government being a mixed one, its democracy might by such an unlimited accession of power, become more than paramount to the other branches, and eventually accomplish their ruin; at the same time that it might, as it appears it did in old times, be attended with tumult and confusion at the hustings. It is sufficient for my argument, to have thus revived a constitutional fact, tending to demonstrate that without disturbing ancient foundations, the base of election may be as widely extended as the best interests of liberty can possibly require.

† The preamble of the act, 8th Henry VI limiting elective franchize to 40s. freeholders, runs thus: 'Whereas the elections of knights of shires, to come to the Parliament of our Lord the King, in many counties of the realm of England, have now of late been made by very great outrages, and excessive numbers of people, dwelling within the same counties of the realm of England, of the which most part was of people of small substance, and of no value, whereof every of them pretended a voice equivalent, as to such electors to be made, with the most worthy Knights and Esquires dwelling within the same counties; whereby manslaughter, riots, batteries, and divisions, among the gentlemen and other people of the same counties, shall very likely rise and be, unless convenient and due remedy be provided in this behalf. Our Lord the King, &c. &c.'

A SECOND act passed, 10th Henry VI requiring that the freehold (to use its own words) should 'lie within the same county where any such choosers will meddle of any such elections.'

Ed{ward}III which expressly says, that they 'shall be holden once every year and more often if need be.' And by Statute 36 of same reign; which declares that they 'shall be holden every year.'

Here then, – our right, even by the written law of the land, and by still more ancient usage, to a very extended elective franchize, and to very frequent Parliaments, is fully proved. They are as noble foundations of a representative government, as any which modern times can boast of.

MAGNA CHARTA. In 1215, we find some of its parts in the great Charter of King John; which was only a ratification of principles in actual operation several centuries before that æra. This charter, in order to prevent arbitrary imprisonment, establishes the principle, that the meanest subject can only be brought to trial, when lawful evidence is given against him. [MAG. CH. *Article* 47]. That his trial must be by jury [*Art.* 48]. It abolishes 'excessive fines,' and also pledges the Crown not to 'sell, deny or defer right and justice' to any man. It also requires that the Prelates, Earls and great Barons, shall be summoned to *the great Council* (afterwards called the Parliament) each by a particular writ: and the lesser Barons, by a general summons of the Sheriff. This charter was deemed so valuable a portion of the constitution, that our ancestors took care to have it confirmed thirty times; that important part of it which secures personal liberty has been corroborated by six different statutes; and all its essential articles were granted to Ireland, in like manner, by Henry III

Even in the few articles which I have now selected, we trace valuable traits of a constitution.

We find it also in the PETITION OF RIGHTS, in the reign of Charles I which renewed and extended THE GREAT CHARTER.[73] Among other matters, it prevents the Crown from obliging the people to grant loans independently of Parliament; it prevents imprisonment without previous cause shewn; it prevents condemnation to death by Crown Commissioners, without trial by the laws and statutes of the realm. So far as this law went, it restored certain parts of the constitution which had been infringed by the monarch.

We find it in the HABEAS CORPUS ACT of Charles II which obliges a jailer to produce in court the body of his prisoner, and shew cause for his detainder. – By it no man can be recommitted for the same offence; which last (Hume says) was a provision for liberty, that had not place in any other government; and those which since that æra have enjoyed it, borrowed it from that constitution which we are now exploring in some of its principal parts.[74]

We find it in the BILL OF RIGHTS, which informs us among other matters THAT neither laws, nor the execution of them, can be suspended by regal authority.[75] – The Star-Chamber, is by it illegal – levying money for, or to the use of the Crown, without grant of Parliament, is illegal – right of the subject to petition the King, declared law; and all commitments or prosecutions for exercising that right, contrary to it.[76] *A standing army* in peace, without consent of Parliament, illegal. Right of Protestant subjects to carry arms, asserted. Election of Members of Parliament ought to be free. Freedom of speech and debate in Parliament, not impeachable; nor to be questioned in any court or place out of the same. Excessive bail not to be required; nor excessive fines imposed; nor cruel, nor unusual punishments inflicted. Jurors to be duly impannelled (not packed); and Juries on charges of high treason, to consist of freeholders. And for 'redress of all grievances, Parliaments to be held frequently.'

The great Whig Commoner, WM. PITT, (not indeed the present gentleman of that name,)[77] mentions one of the principles of our constitution, in the following admirable manner. – 'It is a maxim of our law, that every Englishman's house is his castle. Not that it is surrounded with walls and battlements: it may be a straw-built shed. Every wind of Heaven, may whistle round it; – all the elements of nature, may enter in:– but the King cannot; the King dare not.' – Respecting MAGNA CHARTA, it is a rule that infringements of that charter should not have the force of law. Among other principles, are these; that jurors should be of the vicinage and not composed of men living at a distance. That the duties of the King, to his people, and the allegiance of the people to their King, are reciprocal – That the people may RESIST a Monarch, who endeavours to subvert the religion, laws, and liberties of his subjects; and that although 'to declare war, is the prerogative of the King; to grant or withhold the means of carrying it on, is the privilege of the people, through their representatives.'

I have attempted to enumerate some, among thousands, of the WRITTEN proofs of the existence of a constitution; and of our right to the enjoyment of one, on certain known and fixed principles. But even charters and constitutional statutes, are only testimonies of IMMEMORIAL RIGHTS and PRIVILEGES; and whatever infringes on them should be nugatory and void. Countries long deprived of such blessings, that cannot plead the argument drawn from prescription, naturally fly to parchment declarations, as means of arresting them in their flight. But the claims of Britons and Irishmen, are not only founded on the nature of man, but have been preserved by a living and active principle, which neither the revolution of time, nor the encroachments of regal power, have been able to obliterate from their memories, nor extinguish in their breasts.

The several rights mentioned in this paper, have been occasionally circumscribed; but none of them have been extinguished. The encroachments on the Constitution have proceeded, at one time, from the despotic influence of the Monarch, as in the reign of James II – at another, from the tyrannical and avaricious temper of the people themselves. – An instance of this last kind, we had in the American war. The English, by aiming at unreasonable power, and iniquitous revenue, involved themselves in an immense debt; and in order to pay the interest of it, they have been obliged to give up a share of their liberty, by submitting to Excise laws, (which render an Englishman's house no longer his castle) and to other unconstitutional acts; just as an extravagant individual feels his freedom abridged by his imprudence. These violations of the Constitution, it has generally been the care, and is always the duty of the people to watch with a jealous eye. It is of such abuses that all patriots complain, and seek redress. To the removal of them, they study to direct the attention of the people; knowing from reason, history, and daily experience, that when thus purified, the British Constitution would answer the purposes of good government better, not only than any other that has ever been tried, but than any that has ever been imagined. This is the unanimous sentiment of the patriotic Irishmen, who, on former trying occasions were signalized by their abilities and their virtues. The people have every reason to rely upon the wisdom and the patriotism of such men, and no reason to suspect them of desertion. But there *are* men, whom the people should TRY before they TRUST. – They should place their confidence in the patriots whom I have described, rather than in those persons whom I am going to mention. There are persons who endeavour, in their speeches and actions, to drive things by precipitate and premature violence, to a greater extremity than any one thought of before them; who seem to pay little regard to peace and good order; but speak familiarly of bloodshed and devastation; who laugh at a government that has stood the test of ages, and secured the domestic comfort, the internal quiet, and the personal liberty of the people, as well as extended the power and supported the dignity of the country abroad, better than any other that has ever been heard of. These men trusting to, and insulting your ignorance, throw out certain crude and fantastical ideas, which, instead of being justified by experience, are nothing more than guess-work and conjecture. Among these, is that absurd notion, and notable discovery, that the English have no Constitution. – Now we know, that till lately, the English were the only people who knew what a Constitution meant; that in a political sense even the very word was peculiar to their language, and borrowed from it, by those who lately had no such term, because they had no such idea! – that THEY therefore knew best what it meant; and if others wished to express a different meaning, they should have invented a different word. Such men as these are no more worthy of your confidence, than braggadocios, bullies, or IMPOSTORS of any other class.

Regulate the PRACTICE of our government by its PRINCIPLES; give us Parliaments FREQUENTLY CHOSEN, and REALLY RETURNED *by the great body of* THE PEOPLE, and we shall enjoy all that the wise and good have looked for, or that can ever be found, in FREE GOVERNMENT.

ADDITIONAL NOTES[78]

Sir John Thompson, afterwards Lord Haversham, in his memoirs of the Earl of Anglesey, informs us, that, 'from the 1st of Edward III (1327) to the 14th Henry IV (1412) in the space of 85 years, there are extant 72 original writs for the summons of Parliament; so that allowing 40 days from the tests to the returns of the writs, and but one month for the fittings of Parliament, there will not be a year's interval between the dissolution of one Parliament and the summons of another.' And there are now two laws in force for the *annual* meeting of the King's Parliament, viz 4th and 36th of Edward III.

The early attention of Parliament to prevent the fatal effects of corrupt influence on its members, has been seldom noticed. It appears demonstratively to have been the sense of Parliament in these days, that those who had a vote in granting a tax should have no concern in the collection of it; of course *a Place Bill* is not a novelty in the Constitution. In Edward III it was particularly provided, that 'no Knights of Shires, Citizens, or Burgesses, returned to Parliament, should be collectors for the taxes or subsidies granted to the King.' And when a capitation tax was granted, 4th Richard II (1380) it was also enacted, that 'no Knight, Citizen, or Burgess, of this Parliament, should be collector of this money; but that the King should appoint such as should equally levy it, according to the meaning of the grant, throughout the Kingdom.'

The following spirited reply was given by the Parliament to a declaration of Richard II twelve years before the deposition of that King: viz. 1387.

We have an ancient Constitution; and it was not many ages since experimented, (it grieves us that we must mention it) that if the King, through any evil council, or weak obstinacy, or contempt of his people, or out of a perverse or forward wilfulness, or by any other irregular courses, shall alienate himself from his people, and *refuse to govern by the laws and statutes of the realm*, according to the laudable ordinances, and their faithful advice; but will throw himself headlong into wild designs, and stubbornly exercise his own singular arbitrary will; that, from that time, it shall be lawful for his people, by their full and free assent and consent, *to depose that King* from his throne, and in his stead to establish some other of the royal race upon the same.

Thoughts on the British Constitution
No. VIII[79]

> The History of Greece, by describing the incurable evils inherent in every form of republican policy, evinces the inestimable benefits resulting to liberty itself, from the lawful dominion of hereditary Kings, and the steady operation of well regulated Monarchy.
>
> GILLIES' HIST. GREECE[80]

25 January 1793

At this period of unaccountable revolution in government and sentiment, every mind capable of reflection must be more or less occupied in conjectural anticipation of the event. Humanity revolts at the idea of civil commotion, and fondly embraces every plan, however chimerical, for the extinction of animosity and an union of interests. It is vain, at this enlightened æra, to attempt the conviction of mankind by assertions devoid of argument, but supported by power.

A spirit of enquiry pervades all ranks; it cannot be suppressed. It is now received as an incontrovertible position, that every office in a State should be instituted not for the aggrandizement of individuals, but for *public utility*. By this test every institution is scrutinized. We ask, if one was designed in wisdom; another administered with integrity; a third attended with the advantages proposed?

This mode of investigation is equally tranquil and rational. Abusive establishments must sink under the weight of public opinion, obtained by cool enquiry, and confirmed by reason.

I read with concern the inflammatory publications of wild reformers. They are incapable of appreciating our Constitution. The establishment of a REPUBLIC in a neighbouring nation, from which we have often borrowed sentiments and manners, may reduce to imitation the unreflecting many, and afford a plausible pretext for the malignant activity of the disaffected few; few to the Constitution, but *many* to its Administration.

It is almost needless to display the beauty and wisdom of our Constitution. The advantages of republican, aristocratical, and monarchical governments are happily blended, and many of their defects excluded. The words of the profound and elegant JUNIUS should be emblazoned in letters of gold at this period –

> I can more readily admire the liberal spirit and integrity, than the sound judgment of any man, who prefers a republican form of government, in this, or any other empire of equal extent, to a monarchy so qualified and limited as ours. I am convinced, that neither is it in theory, the wisest system of government, nor practicable in this country. Yet, though I hope the English Constitution will for ever preserve its original monarchial form, I would have the manners of the people purely and strictly republican. I do not mean the licentious spirit of anarchy and riot – I mean a general attachment to the commonweal, distinct from any partial attachment to persons or families; an implicit submission to the laws only, and an affection to the magistrate, proportioned to the integrity and wisdom with which he distributes justice to his people and administers their affairs.[81]

In proportion to my attachment to the constitution, is my indignation at its profligate abuse. That state must be on the brink of dissolution, when its servants deride public opinion, and require no other sanction to their measures than their own venal approbation. Amongst whom, every sentiment of honour and idea of rectitude, are sacrificed to private interest; and who mingle in the usual intercourses of life, without blushing for their depravity, or feeling embarrassed in the presence of unsullied virtue. Popular controul must be purely nominal where the executive power can command a majority for the enaction of laws. – This majority obtained, not by views of public advantage, nor guided by constitutional principles, have made a dishonourable surrender of their judgment for personal emolument.

Is this declamation and an empty parade of words? Let every honest unprejudiced mind reflect. A celebrated historian[82] has said 'the principles of a free constitution are irrecoverably lost, when the legislative power is appointed by the executive.'

Corruption in a free constitution, must be always gradual and imperceptible. The public mind, accustomed to freedom, would repel with indignation every palpable encroachment on their unquestionable rights. – But when oppressed beneath the weight of accumulated corruption, it loses its native energy, and the conscious dignity of independence. Even when the people abandon the spirit of the constitution, they still retain a partial attachment to its forms.

The most detested of the Roman Emperors, disguised their enormities by the formalities of justice. They dignified the senate, to render it an accomplice; and when it had served as the instrument, it became the victim, of their insatiate ambition.

When the body of the people are so far degenerated as to be amused with forms; when their opinion is disregarded and their wishes ungratified by the legislative department; what must be the consequence? I do not wish to anticipate evils by reflection. I think and hope they will be obviated by A TIMELY REFORM. One of the most ardent wishes of my heart, is, that our constitution may be restored to its original purity, without intestine convulsion. Government should remember there is a certain *point of depression*, from which a retrograde motion commences. The people should be instructed, that there are constitutional means of redress; and that when the public mind is fully declared, it MUST be obeyed.

I have often been amazed at the various and opposite opinions of men in private life, concerning the administration of government, who could have no personal interest in perpetuating abuse. One description is styled MODERATE, whose true motive is self-ease; – they think liberty will last their life, and leave posterity to shift for themselves.[83] Another order is denominated LEVELLERS: I believe *their* zeal for reformation proceeds from misinformation. The greater part of mankind have not time to consult the annals of their ancestors, to trace the gradual introduction of corruption, to compare different periods of the same society, and to deduce conclusions of their respective felicity. Tacitus and Pliny were conversant with the productions and characters of Cicero and Cato, and imbibed their zeal.[84]

Thoughts on the British Constitution
No. IX[85]

It often comes to pass, that in governments, where part of the legislative councils of representatives, chosen by the people, that in tract of time this representation becomes very unequal, and disproportionate to the reasons it was first established upon. To what gross absurdities the following of custom, when reason has left it, may lead, we may be satisfied, when we see the bare *name* of a town, of which there remain not so much as the ruins; where scarce so much housing as a sheep-cote, or more inhabitants than a shepherd, is to be found, send as many representatives to the grand assembly of law-makers, as a whole county, numerous in people, and powerful in riches.

LOCKE[86]

15 February 1793

The Author of these Thoughts cannot render more essential service to his country, than by preparing a brief abstract of the several principles of A REFORMED REPRESENTATION, recommended by the highest authorities, and some of them in actual practice in America. The inhabitants of that country, under the guidance of as great and virtuous men as any people were ever blessed with, and well acquainted with the errors that have crept into the British Government, give us a model for improving the representative part of it. This number is dedicated to Mr GRATTAN,[87] and those Societies at present occupied in digesting plans of reform. If it shall furnish a single valuable hint, by bringing under the eye a general view of the several schemes proposed for renovating the Third Branch of our Legislature, the Author will deem his trouble amply rewarded.

EARL OF CHATHAM[88]

Amputation of depopulated boroughs, and an encrease of county members. Speaking of the knights of shires, 'Would to God, (he said) that respectable representation were augmented to a greater number, in order to infuse fresh health and vigour into the sound part of our representation.' In a vein of prophecy respecting *boroughs*, he called them, 'the rotten part of the constitution. It cannot last the century. If it do not drop off, it must be *amputated*.'

DUKE OF RICHMOND[89]

An account of the whole number of males of age in the kingdom (paupers included) is to be taken and divided by the number of members to be sent, which will find the quota of electors, to chuse one member. From the best accounts, it would be in England about two thousand six hundred. These are to be formed into districts or boroughs from the most contiguous parishes, and by having all the elections throughout the kingdom in one and the same day, and taken in each parish, all fear of riots and tumults vanishes.

Compensation made for disfranchized boroughs, as a matter of expediency, not of right.

The present number of members in the House of Commons preserved.

Parliaments annual.

Undecided respecting Catholics voting in Ireland.

Ballot not advisable.

DOCTOR PRICE[90]

Abolition of decayed boroughs.

Compensation to the proprietors of enslaved boroughs, as a matter of expediency. He says, 'The necessity of abolishing such boroughs is very apparent. There cannot be worse nuisances in the state.'

The right of voting extended to all that have property, to a certain value; every county divided into six districts, each of which to chuse one representative, leaving the remaining representatives to be chosen by the largest towns and boroughs.

Roman Catholics of property, to vote in common with Protestants.

Annual Parliaments.

REV. MR WYVILL[91]

Abolition of decayed boroughs. Compensation to every person immediately affected by it; and permission to the disfranchised electors to vote in the counties in lieu of their boroughs.

Right of voting extended to all persons paying taxes in the counties, cities, and boroughs, Roman Catholics included; and to all leaseholders for life, or for a term exceeding 30 years, the yearly value of whose estates shall be at least 40 shillings.

The number of members diminished by the disenfranchisement of boroughs, to be thrown into the counties, the capital, and considerable unrepresented towns.

Annual Parliaments preferable even to triennial.

DOCTOR JEBB[92]

Universal suffrage.

The country divided into districts, each district returning one member.

Or if the former cannot be had, disenfranchisement of some of the boroughs, and compensation. Right of election transferred to townships or districts.

Catholics to vote.

Annual Parliaments.

The constituent body, not the legislative, to form the plan of reform.

LORD EFFINGHAM[93]

Counties and cities to remain just as they are at present.

Counties to be divided into four or more classes, according to their importance in the national scale, considering their population, agriculture, and manufactures.

Each to return from four to ten or twelve burgesses, making in the whole the same number of members as at present.

Every man paying scot and lot, to have a vote for burgesses.[94]

The poll to be taken on a certain day in every parish, before the parish officers and principal inhabitants.

Compensation for disfranchised boroughs.

Ballot not advisable.

Triennial Parliaments.

MAJOR CARTWRIGHT[95]

Universal suffrage. Election by ballot. Annual Parliaments.

HEADS OF A PLAN

Presented to the Dungannon Meeting of 1783, by *the Ulster Committee of Correspondence*, and by them referred to the National Convention.[96]

Decayed boroughs disfranchized; and the diminution of members thereby occasioned, thrown into considerable towns, not at present represented; and into the county, city, and great town representation.

Compensation to the Patrons of disfranchized boroughs, which having had the elective franchize vested in the few, become free cities or boroughs.

Qualification in counties:– Every resident Protestant male (ideots, criminals, &c. excepted) possessed of a freehold of 40 shillings, or any kind of property to the value of 20*l.* over his legal debts.

In cities and towns, like qualification;– also a person having a living in a house for which he pays 5*l.* per annum or upwards.

Menial servants excluded as voters, in county, city, or town, unless they be householders paying taxes.

Voter swears to his qualification, and that he will vote for the candidate he believes most likely to support the liberties of the people in Parliament. Also to take the oath against bribery. Votes once taken, to stand unimpeachable; heavy penalty against a voter falsely swearing, and loss of his franchize.

Members in Parliament (besides the present oaths in use) to swear that neither they, nor any person for them, with their knowledge, bribed any elector to vote for them.

Annual Parliaments.

Election by Ballot.

Extension of suffrage to such description of Roman Catholics as the National Convention should deem proper for that trust.

All elections held on the same day, in the different baronies, half-baronies, or parishes; so as to finish in one or a very few days.

Total exclusion of placemen and pensioners: six public officers allowed to sit in the House, without voting; at the nomination of the Lord Lieutenant.

Plan of the National Convention of Volunteer Delegates assembled in Dublin, in 1783

Decayed boroughs to be opened, by the admission to suffrage of a barony or baronies, parish or parishes, as the case may require.*

Any city, borough, town or manor, (which hath hitherto returned members) shall be considered decayed, that does not now contain a number of electors, over and above potwallopers,[97] not less than 200 in *Ulster*, 100 in *Munster* and *Connaught*, and 70 in *Leinster*. At any time hereafter when such cities, &c. &c. shall so far fall into decay as not to furnish that number of electors, they shall cease to return members until the due number be supplied.

In cities, towns, boroughs, or manors, *not decayed*, (which hath hitherto returned members,) every Protestant, who possesses a

---

* It is observable that the above mode of opening the boroughs was recommended by Mr {Henry}Flood {1732–91, a prominent Irish MP with close links to the Volunteers}, and formed on a precedent within the present reign, of SHOREHAM in England. In 2nd George III (1762.) that borough (in consequence of the great corruption introduced by 'the christian club') was thrown open to the forty-shilling freeholders, in the adjoining Rape of Bramber; whereby 1,200 voters were added; and the borough of CRICKLADE was opened (in 1782) in a familiar manner and for like reasons.

A late valuable publication, the History of Boroughs, makes the following remark on these two cases. 'The practical experiment that has been tried at Shoreham and Cricklade, of the advantages which would attend a Parliamentary Reform, or even a familiar disenfranchisement of the corrupt and decayed boroughs, is a complete refutation of every objection that has been urged against that important measure, as these boroughs have since been represented by independent country gentlemen, and every election has since been conducted with constitutional decorum.'

{*The above section of this note appeared in the original newspaper edition. The rest of this note, from this point, was added when the authors were collecting the essays for publication.*} Mr {George} Ponsonby's {1755–1817} bill of reform, introduced into the Irish House of Commons, in the Session of 1793, and to be discussed in the following Session, adopts the principle of the Shoreham reform, which the National Convention of the Volunteers of Ireland likewise did, ten years before. {See No. XI for a full exposition of this plan}.

freehold interest, yearly value of 10*l.* originally set for 31 years or upwards, and 15 years unexpired at the time, to be a voter in such city, &c. &c. not decayed.

In cities, towns, boroughs, or manors, (deemed by this plan decayed) which hath hitherto returned members; every Protestant who possessed a leasehold, yearly value 5*l.* originally set for 31 years or upwards, and unexpired at the time, to be a voter in such a city, &c. decayed.

In all cities, towns, boroughs, or manors, forty shilling freeholders and upwards, to have votes in such cities, &c.

Non-resident electors in any county, city, town, borough, or manor, not to be permitted to vote therein, unless their right arises from freehold or leasehold property of 20*l.* per annum.

In counties, besides their present electors, persons possessing leasehold interests for years, originally set for 61 years or upwards, of 10*l.* yearly value, and 20 years unexpired, to be voters in counties.

Triennial Parliaments.

Placemen vacate their seats, but capable of re-election.

Pensioners for life, or 21 years and upwards, vacate their seats, but capable of re-election. No other pensioners capable of being returned.

Polls taken for counties, by deputies in each barony.

Elections, *viva voce.*

Abrogation of all corporation bye laws, hitherto made, or to be made, contracting the franchize of electors.

An oath taken by members, against the purchase of votes, also against accepting a pension, during his holding a seat in Parliament, and that he has not accepted one since the test of the writ. A member convicted of perjury respecting this oath, by a jury, to be for ever disqualified for sitting.

Thoughts on the British Constitution
No. X[98]

Continued view of the several Plans proposed, at different times, for
A REFORM IN THE REPRESENTATION of the people in Parliament.

> In being the interest, as well as intention, of the people, to have a
> fair and equal representative, whoever brings it nearest to that, is an
> undoubted friend to, and establisher of the government; and can-
> not miss the consent and approbation of the community.
>
> LOCKE

18 February 1793

Plan of the NATIONAL ASSEMBLY OF DELEGATES, (in their civil
capacity) consisting of five members from each county, city, and
great town, assembled in Dublin, in 1785.[99]

DISFRANCHISEMENT of all cities, towns, boroughs, and manors
in *Ulster*, not containing 300 electors; and in the other three
provinces, not containing 150 electors.

Compensation for extinguished franchize.

The deficiency of members thereby occasioned, to be thrown
into the county representation, and by restoring elective franchize
to the body at large, and adding members to great cities and
populous towns.

Elections by ballot.

Parliaments not to exceed triennial.

Placemen and pensioners vacate their seats.

Residence and registry of voters.

An oath administered to the members against bribery and corruption. – [This is even recommended by *Blackstone*.][100]

MR PITT[101]

When a minister in 1785, moved leave to bring in a bill to amend representation, the plan of which was:

The disfranchizement of 36 of the decayed, or decaying boroughs.

Their 72 members to be distributed to the counties, and such chief towns and cities as are not at present represented.

Compensation to be made to proprietors of such disfranchized boroughs, by a fund of one million of money set apart for the purpose. That their acceptance of the terms shall be by the voluntary act of two thirds of the electors; and not compulsory; but the appreciated value of the borough to be placed out at compound interest.

Right of voting in counties to be extended to copyholders, as well as freeholders.

Mr Fox opposed the idea of compensation to the holders of boroughs, so disfranchized.

Motion lost – 248 to 174.

This plan was approved of by the Revd Mr Wyvill, of Yorkshire, and disliked by the late Dr Jebb.

*   *   *

Mr. Flood[102] proposed the following plan in 1785, in the *Irish House of Commons*:

Annihilation of all bye laws in corporations, that diminish or take away any portion of elective franchize, from persons for whom it was originally intended by charter; to which he said there was hardly a corporation in Ireland that had not been subject.

Every resident Protestant leasehold-housekeeper in a borough or town corporate, to become a voter.

Such leaseholders in boroughs, and all 40 shilling freeholders must be registered and resident: and no freeholder to vote in his county, if non-resident therein, unless his freehold be worth 100*l.* per annum.

Universal registration. For counties, to be done in the baronies.

No non-resident elector in towns corporate or boroughs, to vote in said towns corporate or boroughs, unless possessed of freehold property to the amount of 100*l.* per annum.

County elections to be held in each barony, and all on the same day.

In order to restore population in decayed and contracted boroughs, commissioners to be sent into each county, city, town corporate and borough; to enquire into its particular circumstances, and ascertain the proportion of persons whose votes should return one member. He guessed that the following was about that proportion, viz. In *Leinster*, *Munster*, and *Connaught*, no borough having less than 70 voters, to return more than one representative; and in *Ulster*, no borough with less than 140 voters, to return more than one representative. The diminution of members occasioned thereby, he did not think of consequence; conceiving that it might reduce the number to 240 or 250, instead of the present 300. When the number of voters amount to that specified, then such city, town corporate and borough, shall again return two members as formerly.

In 1790, Mr Flood alleged that there were only two possible modes of amending the representation: by either laying open the boroughs, or adding to the representation of counties.

In that year he moved in the British House of Commons, that 100 members be added to the present number, which hundred to be elected by the *resident housekeepers* throughout the kingdom of Great Britain. He said there must be a very respectable class of people in all countries, especially in England, where every man in the State was competent to pay 50 shillings annually in taxes; and that this would be a body with which Peers and great Commoners would have less influence than on most of them. Mr Fox declared this was the best way of improving the representation he had yet heard of. – A Mr Batley's plan for opening boroughs was, that one or more of the adjacent towns should vote at the elections of members for the decayed place: as a bar against junctions of interest for influencing the returns, and against the probability of the electors being bribed.

A gentleman in Ireland recommended for the improvement of borough representation, that all persons possessed of perpetuities, within the county where the borough or boroughs are, should be allowed to vote. This would be objectionable, as every man possessed of such perpetuity should have a vote in *every* borough in the county, which would be more than he should have. That however may be obviated by forming the county into as many districts as there are boroughs, and allowing only those of perpetuities within each district, to vote for the particular borough contained therein.

REPRESENTATION OF THE CONGRESS OF THE UNITED STATES OF AMERICA

As Agreed to in 1787

CONSTITUTION of *Massachusets*:– Every male of twenty-one years, possessed of a freehold estate of three thousand pounds annual income, or other estate worth 60*l.* votes for a representative in their own assembly. *New York*:– Every male of age, possessed of a freehold worth 20*l.* or renting yearly a tenement value 40*s.* votes for representatives, by ballot; and the qualification of a voter for a member in the senate, is his possession of a freehold of the value of 100*l. New Jersey*:– Inhabitants of age, worth 50*l.* proclamation money, vote for representatives in the senate and assembly. *Pennsylvania*:– Every freeman of age, who has paid taxes twelve months, is a voter. Sons of freeholders to vote, tho' they have not paid taxes. A member incapable of serving in the House of Representatives more than 4 years in 7, and they are chosen by ballot, as are also its delegates to Congress, who are supersedable at pleasure. In this state alone there is not a SENATE, and the executive power is vested in a President and Council. *Maryland*:– Freemen of age, with a freehold of 50 acres of land, vote for the House of Delegates. *North Carolina*:– Senate and House of Commons, both chosen by ballot; freemen of age possessed of a freehold of 50 acres, vote for the members of the Senate; freemen of age who have paid 12 months public taxes, vote for their House of Commons. *South Carolina*:– An elector must be a free white man, of age, possessing a freehold of 50 acres, or a town lot. *Georgia*:– Male white inhabitants of age, possessing a freehold of 10*l.* value, vote by ballot. *Connecticut*:– The old freeholders continue electors. *Virginia*:– Males of age possessing 25 cultivated acres with a house, are voters.

CONGRESS. The legislative powers of the states is vested in a Congress, consisting of a Senate and a House of Representatives. The Senate is elected for six years, the House of Representatives for two. The senators are thrown into three classes: 1st class vacate their seats at expiration of second year; 2d class at expiration of fourth year; and 3d class at the expiration of sixth year – so that one third is chosen every second year. Each state returns two senators, whose qualifications are that they must be 30 years of age, and have been nine years a citizen of the states. A member of the House of Representatives must be 25 years of age, and seven years a citizen.

The whole number of representatives of the states (as well as direct taxes) are apportioned, from time to time, among the different states, according to the number of free persons in each. Enumerations are for this purpose made every ten years, and the number of representatives from a state determined accordingly. They are to be returned at the rate of one to every free persons.

At any time when two-thirds of both houses shall deem the constitution defective, and requiring reform, they may propose amendments in it; or on an application of two-thirds of all the separate legislatures of the states; a convention shall be called for proposing amendments; which proposed alterations shall in either case become part of the constitution, as soon as ratified by the legislatures of three-fourths of the states, or by conventions in three-fourths thereof; as the one or the other mode may chance to be adopted by Congress.

A DELEGATE to Congress cannot hold any office in the gift of Congress, nor receive any salary, fee, or emolument; but they are paid for their attendance by their constituents. No religious test taken by persons holding places of profit or trust.

The President and Vice President hold their places four years, and are appointed by ballot in each state, by a body of electors equal in number to the joint number of representatives and senators returned to Congress by that state; but no person can vote for either of these officers who holds any place himself under the states. The persons for whom the majority of all the states vote, are the elect. The President must be 35 years of age, and 14 years an inhabitant.

*　　*　　*

It appears by the above sketch, that there is not a single state in America which does not require that an elector shall have a qualification of *property*, more or less. In FRANCE the populace were, by their late Constitution, electors, down to very low degree; so low as the payment of about a British half-crown yearly in taxes: and the qualifications for seats in the Assembly itself are not worth mentioning.

Thoughts on the British Constitution
No. XI[103]

Continued view of the several Plans proposed, at different times, for A REFORM IN THE REPRESENTATION of the people in Parliament.

{*No date*}

EXTRACT FROM A PLAN OF REFORM,

Submitted to the consideration of the friends of the Constitution, liberty, and peace, in Dublin,

By one of its Members.[104]

The House of Commons to consist of three hundred members; but the present mode of returning them to cease.

Every person in Ireland having an habitation with more fire-places than one, to pay the tax of 11s. 4½d. – this tax to be distinct from the hearth-money tax, but to be collected by the hearth-money collectors, and payment to be enforced in the manner prescribed, for the enforcing the payment of hearth-money. Where the person paying this tax of 11s. 4½d. is a man of the age of twenty-one years, he is qualified to be an elector. To prevent the word habitation being misunderstood, it means only, what the law deems a man's castle, into which the sheriff cannot make a forcible entry, under any civil writ.

Every person in Ireland, having an habitation with one fire place, and in the actual possession of more than one acre of land, Irish measure, to pay the now hearth-money on one hearth; and to be liable to every other tax. But where such person is a man of the age of twenty-one years, and both his habitation and said land are in the same barony, he is also qualified to be an elector. These two qualifications, above specified, to be the only ones that can confer the elective franchise.

All counties of cities and towns, and every lordship, district, borough, or place, now sending members to parliament, to be considered part of the present thirty-two counties, to which single sheriffs are now annually appointed. Each of such counties of cities and towns, and each of such lordships, districts, boroughs and places, to be henceforth annexed to such of the said thirty-two counties, as the houses contained in them, are reckoned part of, in the return made to the House of Commons, on the 22d of March, 1792, by Thomas Wray, inspector general of hearths.

The three hundred members, in the Commons House of Parliament, to be distributed amongst the said thirty-three counties as follows:

Cork	33 Members	having	76,739	houses
Down	16 do	having	38,351	do
Tyrone	14 do	having	31,814	do
Tipperary	13 do	having	30,793	do
Antrim	13 do	having	30,314	do
Mayo	13 do	having	29,683	do
Limerick	12 do	having	28,932	do
Donegall	11 do	having	24,976	do
Galway	10 do	having	24,268	do
Meath	10 do	having	23,133	do
Armagh	10 do	having	22,900	do

L:Derry	10 Members	having	22,836	houses
Monaghan	9 do	having	21,566	do
Wexford	9 do	having	21,011	do
Kerry	9 do	having	20,213	do
Waterford	8 do	having	18,796	do
Roscommon	8 do	having	18,157	do
Cavan	8 do	having	18,139	do
Clare	8 do	having	18,050	do
Kilkenny	8 do	having	17,719	do
Queen's co.	7 do	having	15,685	do
Sligo	6 do	having	14,962	do
King's co.	6 do	having	14,961	do
Co. of the city of Dublin	6 do	having	14,349	do
Westmeath	6 do	having	13,951	do
Louth	5 do	having	12,827	do
Leitrim	5 do	having	12,378	do
Fermanagh	5 do	having	11,983	do
Wicklow	5 do	having	11,507	do
Co. Dublin	5 do	having	10,759	do
Kildare	4 do	having	10,605	do
Longford	4 do	having	10,348	do
Carlow	4 do	having	8,397	do

The houses herein specified make in all 701,102, agreeable to the return made by Mr Wray, of all the houses in the kingdom, herein before mentioned.

Every elector in the kingdom to give as many votes, as there are members for the county, in which such elector gives his vote. But no man to vote in more counties than one, at any general election. Where however an elector is qualified in more counties than one, he is to have his election, in which county he votes.

The mode of taking the votes, for all the counties, (except the county of the city of Dublin) to be by barony polls, where the high constable of each barony shall preside.

Every man is eligible to be elected, who is not a placeman or pensioner, and every elector may put down the names of such persons, as he pleases, though not declared as candidates.

If any Elector, mediately or immediately, takes, or any candidate, mediately or immediately, gives any bribe, reward, or recompence whatsoever, for or on account of any election, the elector or candidate found guilty thereof, to be precluded from ever voting in future, for any member to be sent to the House of Commons, and to be utterly incapable of ever sitting there himself.

Every man returned to Parliament, to be obliged to serve. He is, however, to receive the sum of 1*l*. 2*s*. 9*d*. out of the public treasury, for every day he attends during the sitting of Parliament.

Triennial Parliaments.

No man to be eligible to be elected into the House of Commons, who is not of the age of twenty-five years, on the day of his election.

Every man taking his seat in the House of Commons is to swear, that he has not directly or indirectly, given any entertainment, bribe, reward, or promise whatsoever to procure his election. That he will not vote for enlarging the duration of the House, beyond the period of this law established. That he will not vote for any form of government, different from that of King, Lords, and Commons. And that he will to the best of his judgment conscientiously discharge his duty in Parliament.

Every member of the House of Commons to be as liable to arrest as any other subject. But where any member of the House of Commons shall remain in actual custody for fourteen days together, during the sitting of Parliament, his seat is to be vacated, and he is to be incapable of re-election, unless he shall be at large on the day of the commencement of the poll. The certificate of two members, of such actual custody, to be, as in other cases, a sufficient authority to the speaker to issue his warrant to fill up the vacancy.

No member to be answerable in any manner, out of the House of Commons, for what he says in it. But where four-fifths of the House agree, any member may be expelled. In case of expulsion, the member expelled cannot sit again in that Parliament.

Any member who shall accept of any place or pension, thereby vacates his seat, and cannot sit again in the House of Commons, while he retains either place or pension. This rule does not however extend in the speaker's salary, nor to the offices of sheriffs and justices of the peace, nor to any office to which there is no emolument annexed.

As no placemen or pensioner can be returned by the people, to the House of Commons, the King or his Viceroy, to have the power of naming seven persons, who are to sit and speak in that House, but not to vote.

As in the course of time, the populousness of counties must vary, a new list of the houses in every county, to be taken once in every twenty-one years, and then the number of members each county is to send to be again proportioned, according to the population of each. But the number of members altogether to continue at 300 and no more.

PLAN OF A PARLIAMENTARY REFORM[105]

The population of Ireland amounts to 4,200,000 nearly. – If the country was divided into 300 districts, nearly equal with respect to population, being collections of parishes, each district would contain 14,000 persons, and might return one member to Parliament.

The number of members of the House of Commons might perhaps be usefully diminished.

If it was necessary to make a bill for reform in a hurry, the division into 287 baronies would answer for the present, with members for the cities and towns.

Each of the 300 districts might be subdivided into 20 inferior divisions, and each of these send five delegates, more or less in proportion to population, to some fixed place in the district to elect the member.

Though there is not the same occasion for this subdivision that there is in France, yet it would be highly useful. The lower classes are better qualified to choose an honest neighbour than to judge of a member of Parliament. In each district of 14,000 inhabitants, there would be at least 2000 voters; and experience has shewn that the votes of such a number cannot be taken without tumult.

All the primary assemblies should meet on the same day.

If two sets of assemblies were not thought necessary, the votes ought to be taken in different places.

The qualifications for voting in the primary assemblies should be –

Residence within the district for the year before.

Registry.

Twenty-one years of age.

Non-voters should be excused from all direct taxes.

There will probably be much variety of opinion on the question of qualification from property.

The following qualifications with respect to property might perhaps answer.

Occupying a certain quantity of a arable land in the country – suppose five acres.

In town, occupying a house of a certain rent, as 10*l*.

The qualification of members of Parliament should be, if any,

Having resided for __ years within __ miles of the chief town of the district, or having been in Parliament before, &c. – A certain age, perhaps 25 years.

The duration of Parliaments might be biennial or triennial, if the duration was fixed; but perhaps it would be better to let the duration be uncertain, to be determined by some method of chance properly secured against tricks.

The manner of voting in Parliament, and in the electoral assemblies should evidently be viva voce, because otherwise their respective constituents could not know whether they deserved to be re-elected. But in primary assemblies it is a question of more difficulty. There is no doubt but that tenants would often vote against their landlords, if they dare. – But on the other hand, it ought to be considered that it is by honest public actions that public principle is chiefly acquired and preserved, without which, no institutions can secure a continuance of freedom. The use of the ballot would give perpetual temptation to falsehood and envy. It is hardly possible to contrive a species of ballot, which shall not be liable to numerous frauds.

A seat in Parliament should be vacated,

By taking a place or pension,

By absence for a certain part of the session.

The House of Commons should be an open court, their proceedings published by authority, and whenever a certain number of members, suppose five, demanded it, the names of those who voted on each side of a particular question should be published.

The members should be entitled to a small salary, such as should barely defray the additional expence of residing in Dublin during the session.

With regard to compensation, whatever is most likely to quiet the country ought to be done. The holders of boroughs have hardly an equitable right to compensation, on the other hand it would be madness to risk commotion about such an object.

If a compensation was determined on, it might be effected in this manner. An act of indemnity should be passed. A committee appointed, before which the property of boroughs should be proved. Those who prove property should obtain debentures to be paid out of a specific fund, which should be the savings of sinecure places and pensions, all of which (except a limited sum for pensions) should go into the public fund at the death of the present holders. In the revenues of sinecure places, I compute a great proportion of the fees of office in several legal offices.

PRINCIPLES OF A BILL

For amending and improving the state of the representation for the people in parliament. Presented by Mr George Ponsonby, 19th July, 1793 – and to be revived in next sessions.[106]

Preamble. – Whereas the state of the representation of the people in parliament is greatly defective, and it would tend much to protect the liberty of the subject, and to preserve our excellent constitution, if the people of this realm were more fairly and equally represented in parliament.

The number of Knights to be elected and returned to represent each county within this kingdom, in any future parliament to be hereafter holden and kept within this realm, to be THREE instead of two.

The number of citizens to be elected and returned to represent the *city* of Dublin in parliament, to be three; and the number of citizens to be elected and returned to represent the *city* of Cork in Parliament to be three.

The power of electing and returning three members to serve in Parliament, confined to each of the thirty-two counties into which this kingdom is now divided, and to the cities of Dublin and Cork, and to no other counties, cities or towns whatsoever.

Preamble. – And whereas enlarging the districts of the several cities and borough towns within this kingdom, would tend to render their elections of citizens and burgesses to serve in parliament, much more free and independent.

The limits or precincts of every city, borough, town or manor having a right to send members to parliament, to extend to a space or distance of four miles from the said city, borough, town or manor, measured by a line to be drawn from some one place within the said city, borough, town or manor, as near the centre of the present scite of the said city, borough, town or manor, as conveniently may be done, and to extend in every direction to a distance of four miles from the said place and no further, so as thereby to make the circuit of the district round the said city, borough, town or manor equal to twenty-four miles in circumference or thereabouts.

Where any city, borough, town or manor, having a right to send members to serve in Parliament, shall be so situate as that a line of four miles cannot conveniently be drawn or measured in the manner directed, by reason of the vicinity of some other city, borough, town or manor having also a right to send members to serve in Parliament, or by reason of the proximity of the sea, then a certain district to be measured from the most central place within the said city, borough, town or manor, in such direction as can be best and most conveniently done, and which shall be equal, or as nearly as may be, to a space contained within a circumference of twenty-four miles, and which space shall be marked out and allotted as and for the district of the said city, borough, town or manor situate as aforesaid.

Every freeholder who shall be seised of a freehold of ten pounds value within the said district of a city, borough, town or manor, shall have a right to vote for members to serve in parliament for the said city, borough, town or manor, any former law or usage to the contrary notwithstanding; provided always, that the said person so claiming a right to vote at said election shall have been seised of his freehold one whole year before the test of the writ which issued for holding the said election, and shall have registered his freehold six months before the test of the said writ, pursuant to the act made in the __ year of his present Majesty, for the due registering of freeholds.

No person elected and admitted to the freedom of any corporation in any city or town corporate shall by virtue of such election and admission, have a right to vote for members to serve in parliament for the said city or town corporate, unless the said person shall have been seised of a *freehold tenement* of the value of *five pounds* by the year, within the said city or town corporate, upon which he or his family shall have resided for one whole year before the time of such election and admission.

Nothing herein contained to extend to any person admitted, or who has a right to his freedom by reason of birth, marriage, or service to any trade or calling, but that all such rights shall remain in full force as if this act had not been made.

Inhabitants of every city, borough, or town corporate, having a right to send members to serve in Parliament, who reside within the prescribed precincts or district of the said city, borough, or town corporate, and who shall have exercised any of the following trades or callings ____ for five years within the districts aforesaid, to from and after the __ day of __ to have a right to vote and be admitted to vote at the election of any representative or representatives to be chosen to represent said cities, boroughs or towns corporate in Parliament.

A member to serve in Parliament from and after the __ day of __ shall before he be admitted to his seat in parliament, take the oath following:

> I do solemnly swear that I have not, directly or indirectly, procured my election and return to parliament by the means of any sum or sums of money, whatsoever, or by any promise of any pecuniary reward whatsoever, and that I have not authorized any person whatsoever to give or promise any sum of money whatsoever for procuring me to be elected and returned a member to serve in parliament, and that if any such promise hath been made on my behalf I will not ratify or make good the same. So help me God.

Provided always, that nothing in this act shall extend, or in anywise be deemed or taken to extend to the cities of Waterford, Kilkenny, Limerick, Londonderry, __ and the towns of __ but that all their rights, franchises and privileges, limits and precincts, shall remain and continue as if this act had not been made.

Thoughts on the British Constitution
No. XII[107]

If it were probable that *every* man would give his vote freely, and without influence of any kind; then, upon the true theory and general principles of liberty, every member of the community, however POOR, should have a vote in electing those delegates, to whose charge is committed the disposition of his property, his liberty, and his life. But since that can hardly be expected in persons of indigent fortunes, or such as are under the immediate dominion of others, all popular states have been obliged to establish certain qualifications.

BLACKSTONE

The misfortune is, that the *deserted* BOROUGHS continue to be summoned.

BLACKSTONE[108]

{No date}

On a review of the several schemes of PARLIAMENTARY REFORM, which in the three last numbers were laid before the public, it will easily be seen that whilst there are certain points on which almost every man differs from another, there are others on which all projectors exactly correspond. These latter, therefore, we shall fairly set down as essential to a reform; whatever other particulars it may embrace or exclude.

Of these essential features of reform, we shall justly consider the disfranchisement, or enlargement, of decayed or close boroughs; as occupying the chief place. In whatever point of view we regard a parliamentary reform, we are struck with the viciousness and absurdity, which vie with each other in this part of the existing system; and we see with a clearness of evidence which renders demonstration superfluous, that no adequate degree of reform can ever be effected, until this mass of political pravity be fully and fairly done away.

On this point, the light of reason bears so powerfully, and all the principles of the constitution point so directly to its importance, that it not only becomes unnecessary to dwell upon it, but we may fairly infer that if the minds of thinking men were not embarrassed by the variety of remedial plans, by the fancifulness of some and the extravagance of others, this political monster must, ere this, even in spite of interested and private views, have fallen a sacrifice to consistency and common benefit.

What then at this day is so incumbent on all these who wish well to a Parliamentary Reform, as to unite their best endeavours for the removal of those obstacles which have hitherto retarded, and unless they are done away, must still retard the attainment of this most desirable object. And how can this be so effectually done as by endeavouring on this important subject, to discriminate between the wild sportings of imagination and the sober operations of reason? How; but by divesting the idea of Reform of every shred of fanatical extravagance, and sending it forth into the world, in the decent drapery of constitutional common sense.

This is the more necessary, because it is only by reducing political opinions to the standard of REASON, that an union of public sentiment can ever be obtained; - and in such an union only, can the Friends of Reform possess that rational force which will supersede and rise superior to every other.

In considering those points on which the various reformers differ from each other, the extension of suffrage strikes us as of the greatest importance.— 'WHO OUGHT TO VOTE FOR MEMBERS OF PARLIAMENT?' To this, therefore, let us direct our attention for the present; and that we may pursue the enquiry with certainty, let us recollect for a moment the real *design* of Parliamentary Representation.

It is the very spirit and essence of the British Constitution, that no law should be made, nor tax imposed, without the consent of the nation. But the nation cannot deliberate. It is impossible for four millions to come together into one place, for the purpose of communicating opinions, weighing reasons, and determining on the best measures. It has therefore been wisely ordained, that the number of persons, freely chosen, should be collected from the different parts of the kingdom, and that to them should be committed the trust of deliberating for the public good; on this obvious principle, that the impartial determination of such a number of persons so chosen, and so collected, may fairly be considered as the unbiassed sense of the people.

Thus, it is evident that the House of Commons is not merely an organ for giving expression to the popular voice – that it is not a registry office for receiving and recording the detail of local sentiments, and giving the name of law to that which may happen to be predominant; but that it is, on the contrary, intended by the constitution to be a great deliberative council, formed of the wisest, the most virtuous, and the most independent men in the country.

Let then the unprejudiced enquirer after political truth ask himself, how this idea of Parliamentary Representation may most effectually be realized – whether by extending the elective suffrage to ALL the male inhabitants of the country, or by limiting it to such persons, as from the possession of some property, have an actual stake in the country, and consequently feel themselves interested in its peace, its liberty, and its prosperity.

In every community it has been acknowledged as a leading political truth, that the exercise of political power ought not to be intrusted to those who were generally unfit to use it for the public advantage; and on this principle, females and minors have been universally excluded; the former being considered as subject to influence – the latter being deemed incapable, from mental immaturity.

Now, if females and minors are justly excluded from the exercise of political power, on the ground of unfitness, it necessarily follows, that where there is an equal unfitness, there ought to be a similar exclusion; and if the principle be an equitable one in itself, it ought, in all justice, and indeed, *a fortiori*, to be applied where such grounds of exclusion meet; in those whose ignorance makes them incompetent, and whose indigence makes them dependent.

It will be understood that I speak of those who have, in strict propriety of speech, no property; who pass thro' life earning their daily bread by their daily labour – but who have *saved* nothing; have made no provision for their families or themselves; for sickness or old age.

That these form a most useful and valuable class of the community, that they have a right to a full share of every political benefit, and that they are even entitled to the peculiar care and tenderness of the higher classes of society, I do most readily grant; – but that they ought to be entrusted with political power, I deny; because it would be dangerous to the Commonwealth, useless to themselves, and inconsistent with every principle of sound policy.

To the exercise of even the lowest political function, some degree of reflection and foresight is indispensably necessary. Without these, he who exercises it, unavoidably becomes either the play-thing of accident or the instrument of design. But reflection and foresight are seldom to be found amongst those who have *absolutely no property*. It is then only, when a man has acquired something, that he looks backward with satisfaction, or forward with solicitude. Till then, he literally takes no thought for to-morrow. He has nothing to lose, he is fearless of danger – and may have something to gain by public confusion.

Cantabit vacuus coram latrone viator.

And yet these unreflecting and improvident sons of poverty, form the great numerical majority of the community. Consequently an unqualified suffrage, would actually throw into their hands the great weight of political power. But in this case who could calculate the consequences? Could we promise ourselves a respectable legis-lature, when the choice should rest with those who are incapable of judging of the necessary qualifications of its members? Could regularity of government be hoped for when the great wheel, which gives motion to the whole political machine, was surren-dered to the mismanagement of the uninformed multitude? Or would it be possible to ensure for any given space of time, the existence of law, of order, of property, of personal liberty, or of personal safety; when the whole fabrick of the constitution were thus absurdly committed to a basis of shifting sand.

Is it necessary to repeat the trite observation, that 'Civil Liberty, when pursued to an extreme, like every other extreme, may merge into its opposite, into despotism;' the worst species of despotism, that of the many; where irresistable power is directed by capricious versatility? Need I remark, that that only is a free government, where reason is paramount; where by a judicious distribution of powers, the few are as safe from the encroachment of the many, as the many are from those of the few; and where national wisdom is kept in unrestrained and regular action for the national benefit.

This, and this only, is genuine liberty. This alone can answer the diversified exigencies of society. – But could this even exist, if the predominance of political power were to be committed to those who can give no security for their conduct; and whose misconduct there would be no means of correcting?

Would the multitude, who should be thus called forward into political action, reap any advantage? Certainly not. Because whatever tends to lessen the stability and regularity of government, must in the same proportion, be injurious to their best interests. It is only under a regular government, growing principally out of *the middle orders* (those true sources of the power, virtue and knowledge of all communities) that the occupations of life, which give employment to the working class, can be carried on with spirit or steadiness. What advantage under heaven, would it be to the day-labourer, to be specifically represented in the House of Commons? Would such a representation, in any degree ameliorate his condition? or could the possession of suffrage secure to the working poor a greater proportion of political advantages, comparatively with the other classes of the community, than they enjoy even in the present state of things? The working poor will then be best represented, when the wisest and most effectual measures are pursued for promoting national prosperity, because theirs is involved in it; for giving encouragement to industry; facility to commerce; and what is absolutely essential to all these, security to property. I say they will then be best represented; because their happiness will then be best provided for, they will be employed more regularly, and they will be paid better. In a free state the higher ranks of society, as they advance, bring forward the lower ones along with them. The progression for instance of the mercantile rank, is felt by the meanest drudge who carries the merchant's bales, from his vessel to his waggon. – But more directly, the thriving influence extends from the merchant to the manufacturer; from the manufacturer to the husbandman – and from the husbandman to the lowest cottager. But can any of these advantages exist where there is not a stable government; and will any man be hardy enough to ensure a stable government, where the whole multitude is brought forward into political action? But how poorly would that multitude be compensated for the loss of certain employment, and perhaps even of the common necessaries of life; by a triennial, a biennial, or even an annual exercise of political power?

If it be said, that the universal possession of the elective franchise is a necessary security against the encroachments of government, I reply, that the security lodged with the individual, should be proportionate to the danger of encroachment. But the difference in this respect, between a man who has *some* property, and him who has absolutely *none*, is almost infinite. It is not personal liberty, but property, against which the abuses of power are chiefly pointed. The political machinery of corrupt statesmen is constructed for one end only – the extortion of revenue. But it is property, to which this machinery must be applied. With property, therefore, in all reason and in all justice, should the counteracting power, in a certain degree be entrusted.

Let no man say that, by an exclusion from this power, the poor are injured. If there is truth in the foregoing observations, they are not injured but benefited; because by this means they are preserved not only from injuring others, but from injuring themselves. If they are injured, it is as the thoughtless youth is injured, whose estate is withheld from him until his mind is matured by experience. – If they are injured, it is an injury which our minors and our females, the hope and the happiness of the community, suffer in common with them.

It is scarcely possible that this exclusion should even in a single instance, have an unfair operation, because it is not likely, that it should extend to an individual, who has the habits necessary for making a proper choice at an election. – For, if the qualification were even higher than it is at present, provided it were extended (as it ought in all reason) to *every* species of permanent property, it would be attainable by every person of industrious and virtuous dispositions, even in the lowest rank. Absolute poverty, in almost every instance, is the result of gross ignorance or habitual misconduct. It is the effect of a moral gravitation, which sinks the subject of it to the centre of the social sphere. Where there is any degree of expansion or elasticity of mind, it shews itself in an effort to rise; and there must be a concurrence of misfortunes, where the effort is unsuccessful. Let us observe real life, and we shall see the truth of this observation fully demonstrated: and what I ask, can be more reasonable, than that the elective franchise should be placed at that point of the scale of society which marks the first gradation of virtuous industry, in its progress from indigence to competency. – At that point, where first the use and value of it can be understood, or the exercise of it be advantageous: – and where it will serve, both as the stimulus to merit, and its reward. And on the other hand, what could be more absurd than to fix it lower – to force it upon those who feel not the want of it, and should not wish for it? who resign themselves without a struggle to that sordid indigence, which they every day see others, (with no greater external advantage than themselves) combat with and conquer! and who, if left to themselves, would be no more affected by the political conflicts which agitate the higher orders of the community, than the torpid shell-fish, which slumbers out its life at the bottom of the ocean, is affected by the fluctuations of the surface.

Thoughts on the British Constitution
No. XIII[109]

It has always been my political sentiment, that it is unjust to attempt to hold a country in subjection, and to govern against the will and opinion of the people.

CHARLES FOX

5 April 1793

That extraordinary meteor in politics, THE FRENCH REVOLUTION, affords an instructive lesson.

It offers demonstrative evidence that even thrones may be insecure, though environed by armed hosts; and points out the policy of seizing on times of profound peace, to revive the principles of rational and temperate freedom. This it urges, as the surest expedient for attaching the hearts of subjects to the laws, securing the strength of their arm against invading foes, and preventing the low murmur of the people from swelling into accents of settled discontent. Though disquiets which have reason for their basis, may be silenced for a season, it is inherent in their nature to gain force by time.

To communities at large, it carries equal admonition. It shews them a point, beyond which their energies cannot be excited, without anarchy; without becoming a bar to those very securities for liberty, which render popular commotion honourable.

In reflecting on the former state of FRANCE, a system of cruelty, monopoly, and abuse, and considering the almost miraculous change that took place; we find an easy clue to the delight with which we contemplated the event.

In their DECLARATION OF RIGHTS,[110] we saw the abstract principles of government revealed, the streams of power laid open to vulgar inspection, and traced up to their source. We were led to view with rapture a new æra in human affairs; which seem'd to promise an enjoyment of civil rights without the slightest alloy, or the smallest sacrifice of the freedom of the individual, to the comforts of regulated society.

When universal liberty seemed within grasp, the prospect was suddenly obscured. The vision was too perfect to be lasting, and the enchantment held but for a day. The things we are hourly witnessing, cannot however pass away without meliorating every soil, in every portion perhaps of the globe; for the germ of liberty will be conveyed to countries that never cultivated it before. Though the utmost sum of theoretical freedom, may not in the issue be attained; all that experience has pronounced rational, practical, and permanent, probably will.

It was natural that an enthusiastic love of Gallic emancipation should widely extend itself, and in no tract of country more than in *the North of Ireland*; that nidus of American Independence, and of liberty to three millions at home.[111] There, the most ardent affection for the late revolution displayed itself; and what heart should have refused to participate?

The recital of facts will revive in our memory the odious scenes which, in the old order of things, were daily displayed in France.

Before THE REVOLUTION, the lives and properties of twenty five millions, were subject without controul to the will of one man. How ill that power was and might be exercised, let the revocation of the edict of Nantz declare; when the galleys were filled with protestants; when five or six hundred thousand men perished in different wars; and a like number (because their religion was not that of Rome,) were forced out of their country, disseminating arts over Europe, many of which were before confined to France.[112]

Letters de Cachet,[113] for the Bastile and other state prisons, were sold with *blanks*, which the purchaser might fill up with names at pleasure; and at his discretion, imprisonment for life in a loathsome dungeon, or to be chained at the oar of a galley, might be the lot of the innocent as well as the guilty. Beside the great Bastile, there were thirty-five smaller ones under other names, in Paris alone.

The liberty of the first subject in the land was at the mercy of a Madame Maintenon,[114] or a Pompadour,[115] or whoever else the King happened to be attached to. Latude[116] might be confined within the walls of a dungeon for thirty five years, or a wretch bruised to death by the carriage wheels of his Majesty's mistress; without the slightest enquiry into the cause of the committal of the one, or the death of the other. The body of an unfortunate man who happened to wound the pride of a courtezan, was 'wasted away in the Bastile with long expectation and confinement. Latude felt what kind of sickness of the heart it was, which arises from hope deferred. On looking nearer, we might see him pale and feverish. In thirty years the western breeze had not once fanned his blood – he had seen no sun, no moon in all that time; nor had the voice of friend or kinsman breathed through his lattice. He was sitting upon the ground on a little straw, in the farthest corner of his dungeon, which was alternately his chair and his bed. A little calendar of small sticks were laid at the head, notched all over with the dismal days and nights he had passed there.' Such was the picture of confinement, drawn by the masterly pencil of Sterne.[117] It was a sketch from nature; and hence the effect it has ever had on the feelings of the reader. The Bastile with its towers, and its fosse, raised those fears which our countryman so well described; and which were felt by every inhabitant of a free country, that has been on the spot. The foundations of that monument of despotism, are now happily rooted out, and grass grows where many a victim has languished from youth to old age, after the very cause of his imprisonment was forgotten, and his prosecutor no more. At its demolition, the electors of Paris found in it and carried away, (to use their own words) 'the ancient arms, frightful by their strange and murderous forms; the chains, so often stained with blood; the shackles, worn down by daily rubbing on the flesh and bones of sufferers for centuries past; and the old corselet of iron, invented to retain a man by all the joints of his body, and to reduce him, like Theseus in Hell, to an eternal immobility.[118] The Hotel de Ville is now in possession of this Chef d'Œuvre, worthy of the Furies, of Phalaris or Cacus.'[119]

Louis XIV at the very moment when he was laying the foundation of a marine to curb the pride of Great Britain, could pass an edict which confined commands in their navy to persons *born gentlemen*, to the exclusion of thousands better qualified perhaps for the charge.

The Marquis de Sillery[120] informs us that within the present century, a General of the army (Marechal d'Estree) received an order of recall, in consequence solely of the caprice of a mistress; in the midst of seventy standards of the enemy, which he had taken possession of, after the battle of Husteimbek.

The torture, with the rack and wheel, in short all the excruciating pains which the most ingenious and diabolical fancy could devise, were inflicted, – viz. burning the hand in the flame of brimstone; pinching the arms, thighs, and breast, with red hot irons; pouring boiling oil with melted lead and rozin into the wounds occasioned by the burning, except those on the breasts which were kindly omitted, lest the loss of life should put an end to further torments; tearing the culprit to pieces at the tails of horses, by means of ligatures upon his arms, legs and thighs, and in the close of the scene, humanely cutting the principal sinews at the joints; the pains of the wretched sufferer prolonged till he had seen a thigh and an arm torn away, when on separation of the second thigh death closed the scene! Of the truth of the most minute circumstance mentioned, testimony was given in a disgraceful detail, *published by authority of the court.*

It is natural to ask in what country, age, and government, this could have happened? – In the polished kingdom of France, in the very reign before the last, and within these thirty six years!! Damiens, who in a fit of lunacy attempted the life of Louis XV[121] was the object of these brutal cruelties, that were among the unhappy consequences of an unlimited monarchy, in which the sovereign was a despot, and his people slaves.

The torture and the galleys were in disuse, and I believe suppress'd in the comparatively mild reign of Louis XVI but that security which turns on the capricious humour of the monarch for the time being, hardly deserves the name. France was a Kingdom filled with court spies. An unguarded expression drop't in places of public resort, in censure of measures of government, or of the favourite or mistress of the King or his minister, often hurried an innocent man from his peaceful home to the deepest cavern of a state prison. Commerce, manufactures, and industry of every kind were held in contempt; and the Janizary,[122] under the name of a French soldier, could insult the most valuable citizen with impunity, and without the formality of a trial for the offence. Within these seven years, at Beauvais, officers were known to attack an audience in a theatre, to wound and kill as many as came within their reach; whilst neither injury nor punishment was considered necessary.

With regard to taxation – The intendant of the taxes upon districts, parishes and individuals, could exempt such persons as he pleased to favor, or diminish the sum. The *Nobility and Clergy* were almost entirely exempted from taxes, tho' best able to pay; and the burthen of all the other orders, particularly the poor, were of course, excessively encreased.

Immoderate *pensions* were lavished on worthless dependants, often without the knowledge even of the King; tho' they were paid out of the hard earned fruits of the people's labour.

Their Nobility consisted of *sixty thousand*. They had *one hundred thousand* privileged persons, all leagued to support their prerogative of paying no proportion of such and such imposts. – *Two hundred thousand* priests reaped, (free of expence,) one fifth of the net produce of all the territorial revenues of that great kingdom, at the same time that they were in possession of immense estates: In one half of the kingdom, tythe gave the Clergy near *a third* of the whole net revenue of the products of the earth; a fourth or fifth in other parts. – Neckar[123] estimated the revenue of the Clergy, at one hundred and thirty millions of Livres, of which little more than forty-two millions were received by the Rectors. Of course eighty-eight millions went to support the pride, splendour, and luxury of an enormous body of pampered prelates; raised on the ruins of the religion of Jesus, and pretending to assimilate with the simple, pure, and unassuming system of the gospel. *Sixty thousand* persons were devoted to the monastic life. The taxes were farmed out for collection, to farmers general, with their army of assistants, amounting to *fifty thousand* more. All offices and commissions, were bought and sold; not even excepting those of the very *magistrates* appointed to decree justice. Patents issued by the court, were bought on speculation by the rich; in order to be sold over the Kingdom, to those who follow the callings of barbers, coal measurers, and even searchers of hog's tongues.

The laws against game were cruel and oppressive, in a degree of which even here we have no conception: the sportsman who dared to kill it, in certain districts, was sent to the Galleys! Their game comprehended wild boars, and herds of deer, not confined to any wall or pale. When the lady of the *Seigneur* chanced to lie in, the tenantry were bound to beat the waters, to keep the frogs silent. Weeding and hoeing the lands were often prohibited, lest the young partridges should be disturbed, and the farmer not suffered by law to use certain manures, tho' best calculated for his grounds; because they affected the flavour of the game. At the *Seigneur's* presses, if he required it, must the farmer's grapes be pressed, and his oven must receive his bread; in order to furnish a pretext for a tax.[124] All the feudal servitude of the dark ages was rigidly exacted: hence the destruction of some *Chateaux* early in the revolution; but still easier is that to be accounted for by the injustice which prevailed in the Seigneur's courts of law.*

The penal code bore no proportion to the nature of crimes; ex. gr. Smugglers of salt, – arm'd, and assembled to the number of five, were in Provence, liable to a fine of five hundred livres and nine years of the galleys; in other parts of the Kingdom they suffered death. Add to these the oppression of their *Gabelles and Corvee*,[125] grievous and impolitic in the extreme. Juries, or any thing that deserved the name of fair trial, were unknown, and when a feeble spark of liberty discovered itself in their Parliaments, the banishment of their members was the consequence, even in the reign of Louis the XVI.

Let who will, fill up the rest of the picture. Enough has been done to vindicate those who had and have virtue sufficient to abhor such slavery wherever found, and to rejoice in every prospect of human beings restored to their natural rights. As to the anarchy, misrule and cruelty at present prevalent in France, he would be

---

* See a late tour through France. {This seems to be a reference to Arthur Young's *Travels in France*, two volumes of which were published in 1792. As further confirmation, notes on Young's work appear in *Joy MSS* 11.}

hardy indeed who should become their advocate. They have arisen from the excess of a virtuous passion, driven to a sad extreme by the weakness, perhaps perfidy, of an unhappy monarch. Forgetting the crimes of a French mob, the magnanimous determination of the French nation in the several provinces of her widely extended domains, no longer to groan under servitude, demanded our admiration; their errors now claim our pity.

Does any man that seriously reflects on these things, wish for a revival of such complicated plans of slavery and degradation? – If there be, let him not call himself christian; for religion teaches us to love one another, and to consider the human race as one family, under the government of the same God. – Does any one who lives in a free country, wish for it? His country may be free, but it is not in the nature of things that he can be so himself; for in his heart he is a slave.

WHAT FRANCE WAS – ENGLAND and IRELAND – may be. How is such a state to be retarded, and the sacred spark of liberty, longest preserved? – By having before our eyes the fall of the ancient Gallic Constitution, the democracy of which was once stronger than our own. – By watching the views of ambitious men, and taking every fair opportunity of bringing our own constitution back to its *first principles*. Tho' this is to be done with a deliberate hand, no difficulty should alarm us, nor cause it to be neglected.

With respect to our own country, the imperfect state of parliamentary representation, and the gradual inroads of power, upon the best and most ancient mounds of the constitution, may have produced in some of the chastest breasts, a momentary admiration of forms of government more pleasing to the eye than our own, but no less subject to abuse, nor less grievous in their decay.

General Assemblies of the people have, however, in all quarters, reprobated republican ideas, by DECLARATIONS energetic and strong, in exact ratio with the magnitude and respectability of the meeting. From the commons collected in a Barony or a County, to one million four hundred thousand inhabitants represented in a province, at *Dungannon*,[126] expressions of unbounded affection for their Prince, and of love for their constitution in its true principles, have risen in such a climax of loyalty, as to leave the enemies of reform without one solitary pretext for avoiding a fair discussion of the grievances of the subject. But it is not the power of *the Crown* of which good men complain, tho' the venerated name of Majesty is in every interested man's mouth. It is the encreased, encreasing, and undue power of the *Aristocracy*, which in progress of time may destroy the Regal Branch itself.

It has been the chief design of these THOUGHTS to turn public attention to *the theory* of the British constitution, and to some of its most ancient *principles*, as points for shaping such a course as may avoid the rocks surrounding unlimited Monarchy, and democratical Tyranny; and lead to that happier mean which lies between both.

DOES GREAT BRITAIN OR IRELAND FULLY ENJOY THAT CONSTITUTION which these papers hold up as a pattern of unrivalled excellence?

The following Questions will determine.

I. Are the laws affecting life, person, and property, framed with the consent of the King – the Lords – and the commons; the last fully and fairly represented in a third branch of the Legislature? [General suffrage of all freemen present, the ancient practice; confirmed by statute 7th, Henry IV – but restricted to 40s. freeholders by 8th Henry VI –*]

II. Are Elections and Members of Parliament FREE? [*Bill of Rights.*]

---

* The reader cannot imagine that *universal* suffrage, is recommended by this reference to ancient practice; as the opinion of the author was explained on that point in number *eleven* {Note that No. XI of the original newspaper essays, referred to here, is actually found as No. XII in the collected edition.}

III. Can no man be imprisoned without previous cause shewn? [*Petition of Rights*, Charles I]

IV. Can a subject (except in particular cases which the law has long declared) insist on the benefit of a Habeas Corpus; and must a jailor produce in court the body of his prisoner, and shew *cause* for his detainder? [*Habeas Corpus*, Chas. II]

V. Can the meanest subject be brought to trial only when lawful evidence is given against him? (*Magna Charta*, chap. 47, John.)

VI. Must *every* alleged crime be tried by a *Jury*, consisting of the Peers of the accused, resident in the vicinage? – (*Magna Charta*, chap. 48.)

VII. Is it impossible, from the nature of the law respecting Juries, that they can be unduly impannelled, or *packed*, in any case whatsoever?

VIII. Can excessive fines (disproportioned to the offence, or to the ability of the person to pay them) never be exacted? (*Magna Charta*.)

IX. Can no power in the State exact excessive bail? – (*Bill of Rights*.)

X. Is a man's house still his *castle* – tho' 'a straw built shed,' and tho' 'every wind of Heaven may whistle round it, and all the elements of nature enter in.'? (Lord Chatham, and the ancient practice of the constitution, prior to excise and certain other laws.)

XI. Can neither the Crown, nor its servants, sell, deny, or defer right and justice to *any* man? (*Magna Charta*.)

If these are already enjoyed; if the benefits of the great Charter, of the Petition of Rights, of the Bill of Rights, and the several guards of our liberties confirmed at the Revolution, are still in undiminished force, let every man sit down contented under his vine, happy in the reflection that his country is free. But if they are not; the talents of the wise and the hearts of all, should be engaged in their attainment – because the points enumerated are essential in the British constitution. No abuse in the practice of that con-stitution, can however be charged to the principle; We may lament and strive to remove the one, but we should never cease to venerate the other.

In no possible situation should the people of this or any country, or age, be tempted to despair. – When the cup is even ready to overflow, comfort is at hand. It is one of the means of Providence, for preserving a balance in human affairs, that the very enormity of an evil shall contribute to its cure.

Thoughts on the British Constitution
No. XIV[127]

The total disuse of arms amongst the lower classes of people, laid that opulent country (Carthage) open; an easy and a tempting prey to every invader. This was another capital error, and consequently another cause which contributed to their ruin. How must any nation, like our own, (*England*) which with respect to the bulk of the people, lies in the same defenceless situation; how, I say, must they censure the mighty State of Carthage, spreading terror and giving law to the most distant nations by her powerful fleets, when they see her at the same time trembling and giving herself up for lost, at the landing of any invader in her own territories?

MONTAGUE; ANCIENT REPUBLICS[128]

13 August 1793

It is a principle of the British constitution, that every freeman should be armed. This is equally his right, and his duty. It is a privilege which tends to secure the possession of every other, against both foreign enemies and domestic tyrants; and he is therefore under an obligation to exercise a right of so much consequence to Society.

This principle has been handed down to us from the remotest antiquity. Notwithstanding the unconstitutional tyranny of game laws,[129] and the restrictions imposed on *Roman Catholics* in times of jealousy and dissention, it is at this moment exercised in an eminent degree: and it is to be hoped that the people of this country will never suffer their right to be infringed.

The practice of carrying arms, must necessarily rank among the first, in point of time, that obtained in every civil society: – but we know, in particular, that it was an essential duty in feudal times. It was even the condition upon which both Lords and Commons held their lands. Hence, their titles to their property, were called Military Tenures.

So thoroughly was this principle established, when the Barons extorted Magna Charta from John in 1215, that it was thought unnecessary to mention it among their privileges. That it was the duty of the people, was plain to every one; for they not only held their estates by military tenure, but were frequently called into the field by their respective chiefs. That it was their right, could not be doubted at Runnemede, where the Barons, with their tenants were encamped in defiance of the King.

It is unnecessary to seek for proofs of this practice in the four succeeding centuries, because the same system continued; and previously to the establishment of standing armies, wars were carried on by the proprietors of land.

When the establishment of standing armies had rendered the people remiss in performing this duty to their country; and justly excited the jealousy of Parliament – it was thought necessary to remind the King of the rights of his people, and to remind the people of their duty. We accordingly find articles to the following purport in the BILL OF RIGHTS, 1689 –

– That the raising or keeping a standing army within the kingdom, in time of peace, unless it be with the consent of parliament, is against law.

– That the subjects which are Protestants, may have arms for their defence, suitable to their condition, and as allowed by law.

The distracted state of this kingdom induced the government, at several periods, to enforce the obligation of bearing arms upon the English and Scotch settlers, under heavy penalties; – and in the *City of Dublin* in particular, the oath of a freeman binds him, at this day, to be furnished with such armour and weapons as were in use when the oath was framed.

That this liberty of having arms implied the liberty of ARRAYING and EXERCISING IN BODIES, is evident even from such considerations as these:– THAT if a man be allowed to have arms, he must be permitted to learn their use; otherwise the permission would be nugatory: THAT if two or more citizens be attacked, the law must necessarily authorize them to co-operate for their mutual defence: THAT if a neighbourhood, or town, be exposed to danger, the inhabitants must unite, and learn to act together, or their arms would be useless; and a few riotous persons, or a banditti, might pillage each house separately, and murder the family without interruption: THAT if the country be threatened by foreign or eternal enemies, the people must act in concert, and take the most effectual method of making resistance. AND THAT this cannot be done without providing uniform arms, and accoutrements, nor without being regularly disciplined and commanded.

But beside these general considerations, we are supported in this opinion by the constitutional facts already mentioned. For, 1st. Perhaps a principal motive to the formation of societies, was reciprocal defence and co-operation. 2d. In military times, the people were bound by their leases, to embody, when the kingdom was in danger either from abroad or at home. 3d. The armour and weapons with which the freemen of cities were required to be furnished, would have been of little use, except in battle array. And 4th. THE BILL OF RIGHTS could not mean to leave any doubt of the constitutional conduct of its authors, who had recently exercised this right in effecting *the Revolution*.

If any person should still hesitate upon this point, his mind must be fully convinced by what has passed in our own times: for we have seen this principle of common law declared in the most solemn and deliberate manner. We have seen both houses of parliament returning thanks to numerous bodies of citizens, regularly armed, disciplined and embodied, without receiving pay or any other aid, or acknowledging any military subjection to the executive power. Nay his Majesty himself intimated his concurrence with the Lords and Commons, by receiving a deputation from the Volunteers of Ireland.

It is incontrovertible, that the recent improvement made in the constitution of Ireland, and the extension of her trade, as well as her security from *invasion* during the American war, are to be ascribed to the discipline of the Volunteers, and to the formidable bodies which learned to act together at Reviews: for had every individual stood alone, the people would have been only the more despised on account of their simplicity, in providing themselves with arms which they were incapable of using. The approbation of his Majesty and the two Houses, was not therefore conferred upon them as individuals; for as unconnected individuals, they could not have effected any of the purposes for which they received this approbation. It was given to them as an army, which had equipped itself for actual service, without requiring any assistance from government.

Still, perhaps, some timorous persons may be prevented from yielding to the force of these arguments, by their fears. They may think that government could not be carried on, if all the people were armed. In my opinion, this is the very circumstance which renders the Volunteer associations all-powerful in *acting right*, and impotent in acting wrong. If indeed only a certain description of the people were armed, they must become formidable both to government, and their fellow-citizens. But when the Volunteers and the people are in fact the same body, it is plain that the people have nothing to fear, and it is equally evident that government is safe from being over-ruled by a faction. If indeed a whole nation in arms, should concur in demanding a redress of grievances, and an administration should refuse to comply; it might then tremble; and who is there that would have it otherwise? Were all the people on one side and their servants on the other; the people would command, and their servants must obey. But in the regular course of affairs, when government studies the interest of the nation, the nation being armed will take care that they shall meet with no obstruction in the discharge of their duty; no petty insurrection will dare to shew its head; no formidable rebellion, to raise its crest.

It is the interest of every well meaning government, that our military association should flourish even in time of peace; but on the eve of a war, it would be madness or treason to discourage them. Administration should then solicit their assistance, for they are the only force which can protect the country, by land. How could IRELAND be protected from a *French invasion* by 12,000 men, effectives and non-effectives, cantoned throughout the kingdom; a great part of them necessary for garrison duty, and for the execution of the laws? SHE MUST THEN DEPEND ON THE VOLUNTEER ARMY; inexhaustible in point of numbers, quartered in every parish, intimately acquainted with the country, and equally interested and intrepid in the defence of their liberties.

*   *   *

The following Extracts are made from Irish acts of Edward the Fourth, rather as matter of curiosity, than as connected with this publication.

STATUTE V. OF ED{WARD}. IV. CHAP. IV.

An act that every Englishman, and Irishman, that dwelleth with Englishmen, between sixty and sixteen in years, shall have an English bow and arrows.

Rot. Par.[130] Cap. 17.

Item. At the request of the Commons that consideration had to the great number of Irishmen, that exceed greatly the English people, that in force and augmentation of the King's lieges, it is ordeyned by the same parliament that every Englishman and Irishman that dwell with Englishmen and speak English, that be between sixty and sixteen in age, shall have an English bow of his own length, and one fist meal at the least betwixt the necks, with twelve shafts of the length of three-fourths of the standard; the bows of yew, wych, hassel, ash, awburn, or any other reasonable tree, according to their power, and the shafts in the same manner, within two months next after the publication of the estatute, upon pain of two pence a moneth, from moneth to other, for that he shall have and continue the bow and shafts, and in lieu of the bow and shafts broken and lost to have new under pane of two-pence every moneth till it be done, and yet not prohibiting gentlemen on horseback to ride according to their best dispositions, to ride with spear, so that they have bows with their men for time of necessity.

CHAP. V.

An act for having a constable in every town, and a pair of butts for shooting, and that every man betwixt sixty and sixteen shall shoot every holyday at the same butts.

Rot. Par. Chap. 18.

At the request of the Commons it is ordayned and established by
authority of said Parliament, that in every English town of this
land that pass three houses holden by tenants, where no other
president is, be chosen by his neighbours, or by the Lord of the
same town, one constable to be president and governor of the same
town in all things that pertain to the common rules of the same
town, as in ordinance of nightwatch, from Michaelmas to Easter,
yearly, under pain of three pence every night; and also to ordayne
one pair of butts for shooting within the town, or well neere, upon
cost and labour of the said town, under pane of two shillings from
one moneth to the other, from the publication hereof till the
constable be made, and the butts also, and that every man in the
same town in such hour as the constable, or his deputy of his
neighbours shall assign, that is, between sixty and sixteen, must be
before the constable, or his deputy, at the same butts, and shoot up
and down three times every feast day betwixt the first day of
March and the last day of July, under pane of *one half-penny* for
every day, and that all these panes be levied off their goods or
wages from moneth to moneth by the constable, to be spent in the
strengthening of the same town, or otherwise in his default to be
levied by the wardein of the place, and that the panes be spent
upon the towns when the said panes riseth.

Thoughts on the British Constitution
No. XV[131]

The Democracies in this quarter of the world are inconsiderable in power; but, if that tumultuary form of Government should be re-established in great States, and popular Assemblies again entrusted with executive functions, ought not the principles established in this discourse to convince us that such assemblies would abuse power *now*, as grossly as they did formerly? Is it not to be dreaded that the ancient barbarities would be renewed, the manners of men again tainted with a savage ferocity, and those enormities, the bare description of which is shocking to human nature, be introduced, repeated, and gradually become familiar?

GILLIS'S LIFE OF LYSIAS AND ISOCRATES[132]

12 April 1793

The British Constitution has been sometimes compared with NEW OR IMAGINARY Republics. – It may not therefore be inexpedient to compare it with those Republican Forms of Government which we know to be ancient, and to have been reduced to practice. A complete contrast would indeed be impracticable in the space and time allotted to publications of this kind. All that can be aimed at is to suggest a few hints, which may induce my readers to prosecute the same train of thoughts.

From the pacific declarations of the French Republic,[133] tho' not yet verified by experience, it has been concluded that if all European States adopted the Republican Form, *wars* would cease – and the frequency of hostilities among modern nations has been ascribed to their Monarchical Governments. – How such an idea should enter the head of any man who had ever read history, is to me altogether unaccountable; for every one knows that SPARTA, ATHENS, and above all, ROME, were the most restless, ambitious, and warlike states even of ancient times; and that there is not one modern nation that can stand in competition with them in this respect. It is not necessary, however, to seek for examples beyond GREECE; for the ancient state of that country is a case in point. Were *Europe* covered with Republics, she would be a second Greece, on a larger scale; and the incessant and desperate contests which were supported by those ancient states, would be renewed; with this difference, that hostilities would last longer, and be more destructive. The Commonwealth of England was scarcely formed, when it engaged in a desperate war with the *Republic* of Holland: and the Cantons of Switzerland have supplied every state in Europe with troops. Republics therefore are fond of war. Nor should this propensity appear strange to any one; for the cause of it is very obvious.

In BRITAIN, where the prerogative of war and peace is vested in the King, we know that though an inglorious peace may sometimes be concluded, and an imprudent war declared, there are many obstacles in the way of both the one and the other. A regard to the sense of the public, and particularly of the two houses, is even at this day a powerful restraint; as we have repeatedly experienced within a few years, particularly in *the Russian armament*:[134] and as neither the King nor his principal advisers, are military men, the mad passion for *military glory* can have little influence.

But in Republics, it is easy to enflame the resentment, the avarice, or the ambition of a popular assembly; and there is always a number of demagogues and desperate swordsmen, whose passion is fame, and whose interest is best promoted by public confusion and foreign wars.

Now if wars would continue under Republican forms, it is plain that they could not be carried on without *standing armies*. Some of the ancient Republics were military communities. The Citizens were not only soldiers, but they were nothing else. ROME and SPARTA were *garrisons*; from which drafts and detachments might be made without any material change in their mode of living; nay sometimes, actual service was esteemed a relaxation from duty, and a lucrative employment. But in the tranquil, commercial state of modern Europe, the inhabitants would scarcely brook to be ordered into camp, and would think it a strange commencement of Liberty and Equality; to be transported for seven years to *Gibraltar*, *Africa*, or the *East Indies*.

Standing armies, therefore would *still* be necessary; and a little reflection will convince any man that they are more formidable in Republics than in Monarchies. ROME, it is well known, was frequently overrun, and at length destroyed, even by an army of her own children. Her rival CARTHAGE, which like *England* was a commercial state, and found it cheaper and easier to *buy* soldiers, than to fight her own battles, was brought to the brink of destruction by an army of foreign mercenaries – In the time of CROMWELL, the English Commonwealth was governed by a *council of officers*; and from after, the army of the Commonwealth restored Charles II without condition or stipulation. The long Parliament was as able and virtuous a body of men as ever sat in any Senate: yet the result of their efforts, was military tyranny and Cromwellian usurpation; rendered hereditary in the person of Richard Cromwell, and suppressed only to make way for the profligate and licentious Charles.

From these facts it will also appear that European Republics cannot be exempt from TAXES. A popular Government may no doubt be conducted at less expence than a Monarchy; but when a National Assembly, a standing army, a powerful navy, and frequent wars are to be supported, in addition to the ordinary expences of Government, – the people must be subject to heavy imposts. America indeed is happy in this respect; but it is owing to her remote situation. Yet even America, though without army, or navy, is subject to many taxes, particularly a heavy Excise, which even now is exciting discontent.

As I have shewn, that a *modern Republic* would probably be a *warlike state*, and consequently liable to the despotism of a standing army, and subject to grievous taxes; so it might be easily shewn that it would be less able to bear these burdens than such a kingdom as England: for COMMERCE is not congenial with a Republican Government.

The stability of a Republic depends on a considerable degree of equality among the citizens, in point of property. This can be maintained only by discouraging commerce; by Agrarian Laws; by violating the right of a man to bequeath his property; or by familiar contrivances, which have actually been recommended by some popular writers. A state in which such a disparity of wealth exists as is to be found at present in England, could not long continue under a Republican Government: and this disparity would soon take place in a free commercial country. It is probable, then, that extensive and prosperous commerce would be fatal to a Republic. Now, we all know, that in England, on the contrary, Commerce was the parent and nurse of liberty.

It has been already observed, that democratical Governments are peculiarly exposed to the storms of FACTION. 'Of all the states of Greece,' says Montague, 'Athens' which was the head of the democratical confederacy 'may be most strictly termed the seat of faction.'[135] But they are subject to a greater evil than this – I mean the effects of foreign intrigues and bribery. It is the nature of democratical Republics to be influenced by men of popular talents, who are often in indigent circumstances. A very small sum may be a great object to one of these Demagogues: and his friendship may be of immense value to a state which is carrying on war, or negociating with his country. To expect that such temptations will be resisted, or to imagine that a popular assembly may not be deluded by an artful leader, is to declare profound ignorance both of modern and ancient times.

This is the side in which FRANCE will be most easily wounded; and if her government continue in its present form, it is probable she may, in time, fall a victim to foreign influence, and domestic treachery; for every European state may have agents in her assembly, who will either sacrifice her interests to their employers, or occasion such general distrust in the nation, that they will be hurried into some desperate expedient as a cure for their distractions – as actually happened in *England* at the RESTORATION.

Those who have most strenuously objected to any arguments drawn from the *Theory* of the British Constitution, have very inconsistently argued from *abstract* democratical notions, that have never been put in execution. In this paper I have set aside both THEORIES, and appealed to EXPERIENCE. From experience it has appeared, that an European Republic would naturally be restless, factious, ambitious, and exposed to frequent destructive wars; and these must be conducted by standing armies and navies; that these will require high taxes in addition to those which are necessary for the internal government; that without commerce, it will be unable to support such burdens; and *with it*, the people will soon become, by inequality of property, unfit for a democratical constitution: and finally, that beside the consequences of intestine divisions, its interests will be continually BETRAYED TO ITS ENEMIES.

Thoughts on the British Constitution
No. XVI[136]

> That people (the Athenians) highly susceptible, as they are, of lively and transient sensations, stand distinguished beyond all other nations, for uniting the most discordant qualities, and such as may be most easily abused to mislead them.
>
> ANACHARSIS[137]

30 April 1793

It is very observable that the writer who lately acquired the greatest ascendancy over the public mind, drew nothing from HISTORY.[138] This must have been occasioned either by ignorance, by a desire of imposing on their readers, or by an opinion that we are not only wiser than all our predecessors, but so well acquainted with the principles of politics, that we cannot derive any benefit from their wisdom, or experience. Ignorance or imposture, it would be uncivil to impute: nor can we charge them with such self-sufficiency and presumption as are implied by the last supposition, without suspecting them of the greatest absurdity – for every wise man knows that he may receive advantage from the knowledge of the success, the misfortunes, and the observations even of a weak one. Yet, upon this idea, seems to be founded that common notion, so favourable to indolence and ignorance, that A NEW ÆRA has commenced, that Governments are in future to be constituted upon maxims entirely new, and that the facts recorded in History cannot apply to Constitutions which bear no resemblance to ancient forms of Government.

It is said in particular, that a Legislature PURELY REPRESEN-TATIVE, is a modern invention, and of course that none of the observations drawn from the *old* Republics are applicable to it. If this plan were indeed so recent as it is said to be, it would be very liable to suspicion, for it would come under the description of an experiment; and people would naturally prefer a government which had, for a great length of time stood the test of experience, to a mere novelty.

But in fact it is not a novelty. Representation has had a share in many Constitutions: and there is in ancient history an instance of a pure representative democratical Republic, which is nearly the counterpart of the plan lately submitted to *the French*. – This Republic is ATHENS, from which many of the observations in former numbers of these thoughts have been drawn.

Since the political system lately introduced into France is considered by many as a new discovery, it may not be unseasonable to point out the particulars in which it resembles the Grecian policy: and since it is looked upon as a contrast to the imperfect form of Government established in ENGLAND, it cannot be irrelevant to the intention of this publication, to state the effects produced by this plan upon a people who have always been thought to bear a remarkable resemblance to the French. It is obvious that upon such extensive subjects, a few hints must suffice. A full discussion would fill a volume, and might laudably employ the pen of some eminent scholar and politician.

In ATTICA[139] as in FRANCE, the Sovereignty resided in the people; who claimed and exercised the right of acting in their collective capacity, as often as they thought proper. But as the administration of public affairs could not be conducted by so numerous a body, they vested the powers of Government, in ordinary cases, in a Senate. In Athens however, the interference of the people was much more frequent than in France, in consequence of the very confined limits of its territory.

The people, that they might perform the functions which they reserved to themselves, were divided into certain districts, called DEMOI. Of these there were in Attica 174. They may be compared to the *Communes* or *Sections* in France.[140]

Each Section was under the direction of a set of Officers called DEMARCHS. It was their business to assemble the inhabitants on public occasions; to keep a registry of the Citizens resident in the district; to preside at the election of Senators and Magistrates, &c. In all these respects they bore an exact resemblance to the *Bureau de l'assemblée primaire*.[141]

At these elections in both countries, the poorest citizens were capable of electing, and being elected; except they had been precluded by conviction of certain crimes. The meanest citizens were eligible to the highest offices: and foreigners when naturalized, had all the privileges of citizens. In the admission of new citizens, however, the Athenians were stricter than the French. The electors of course were more select in Attica than in France, even after the time of ARISTIDES,[142] who extended the privileges of the lower orders; and the candidates were subject to a severe scrutiny, before they could be proposed.

The Districts of Attica were classed under *ten tribes*, answering to *the Departments* of France;[143] each of which appointed fifty representatives to the Senate. The members for each tribe, formed a committee, and every committee in its turn presided for 35 days over the affairs of the State, during which time it was called the PRYTANY. Ten deputies of the committee constituted a *sub*-committee, who were stiled PROEDRI, held their office for a week, and seem to answer to the French *Executive Council*.[144] One of their number presided every day; and was also president, or EPISTATES of the Senate.

The *Senate*, like the *Legislative Assembly*,[145] exercised a considerable share of the executive Government. – It's members must have attained the age of thirty years, previous to election. They sat every day; and to guard against vacancies, the people of the *Primary* Assemblies appointed EPILACHONS, or *Suppleans*, as substitutes for those who might die or be expelled.

The SENATE, like the *Legislative Assembly*, was elected annually; and the deputies received daily wages. It might make decrees, which continued in force for a year; and in ordinary cases, it had a previous negative on the deliberations of the people, but its more important acts were submitted to the General Assembly for sanction; as the French *Assembly* refers matters of singular moment to the *departments*. – Upon this part of SOLON's plan,[146] the Scythian philosopher[147] shrewdly observed – that in Athens *wise* men were to deliberate, and *fools* to decide.

The free citizens of Athens were not as numerous in proportion to the rest of the inhabitants as those of France, but they were more fully represented; for beside their personal attendance in the Assembly of the people, there was a representative for every forty citizens.

Lastly, the same distinction took place between *decrees* and laws, in each state. – 'A *law* is distinguished by its universality and its indefinite duration. A *decree* is confined to a certain district, particular individuals, or a limited period of time.' – [French Constitution – Tit. VIII. § II. 4.]

All magistrates, and other public officers, were chosen annually as in France, by open suffrage, ballot, or LOT. The last mode of deciding among the candidates, was very common; and probably arose from long experience of the caprice or corruption of the multitude.

Some of these, after having discharged the highest offices in the state, with unquestionable wisdom and integrity, were admitted into the court of AREOPAGUS,[148] for life.

Other magistrates presided as judges in different courts, while they were in office.

All judges therefore were *elective* as in France; and like the French ones were assisted by JURIES.

The jurors were very numerous, often 500; and on some occasions, even *six thousand*; and received compensation for their attendance.

Some of the judges went circuit, and resembled *Les Censeurs Judiciares*.

Should the parties choose to decide their difference by arbitration, their right to do so is expressly ascertained in both constitutions.

The EUTHUNI of Athens corresponded with *le Bureau de Comptabilité*, or commissioners of accounts in France.[149]

These are some of the principal points in which these two forms of government coincided. It would be easy to mention others in which they differed, and in which the Athenians had the advantage – according to the modern system of politics.

Thus the mass of the people more frequently acted *in person*. The representation was more complete. – The EPISTATES, or president of the Senate, and principal officer of state, held his office but *one day*, and could not be chosen a second time.

There is another circumstance in which the Greeks were superior – 'It is a great advantage,' says an enlightened French author, 'that the nature of the Democracy (Athens) rendered delays and enquiries necessary, in matters of legislation:' but he subjoins an observation equally applicable to both – 'it is often a great misfortune that they are no less unavoidable on occasions that call for celerity and dispatch.' – Barthelemi.[150] Le peuple a toujours trop d'action, ou trop peu. Quelquefois, avec cent mille bras, il renverse tout; quelquefois avec cent mille pieds il ne va que comme les insectes. Montesquieu, *Esprit de Loix Liv.* II. *ch.* 2. – The people have always either too much activity, or too little. Sometimes, with an hundred thousand arms, they overturn every thing; sometimes with an hundred thousand feet, they crawl like insects.

These remarks will satisfy the reader, that *the French constitution is not a singular phenomenon*. Now if this plan was formerly carried into execution – the next question that arises is, HOW DID IT OPERATE? – From its past operation, we may form conjectures concerning its future effects. The result of a *second* trial may be more or less favourable than the first, in a certain degree, according to the character and situation of the people upon whom it is made: but while mankind continues the same species, the events of similar experiments cannot essentially differ.

Attica, as well as France, was originally under a kingly government. It adopted the republican form, for a very whimsical reason. CODRUS, their last King, was so good, that they determined never to have another.[151]

The constitution of Athens was scarcely formed, when PISISTRATUS, by his popular talents, obtained an absolute ascendancy over the people, and left his sons in possession of the supreme power.[152]

Though they were dispossessed by a second Revolution, the history of Athens is, in a great measure, a history of demagogues, who successively exercised all the powers and commanded the treasures of the state; as the history of an absolute monarchy is little more than an account of its Kings. Some of these were men of transcendant abilities and virtues: but others were distinguished only by a profligate audacity. CLEON and ALCIBIADES, were equally powerful, with THEMISTOCLES and ARISTIDES.[153]

Some of these great men were injuriously suspected of being subservient to foreign powers, and others of a class inferior in talents, tho' not in influence, we know to have been *bribed*.

Between a mean distrust of the best citizens, and a blind confidence in base declaimers, the state was incessantly distracted by hostile factions. This spirit of jealousy at length arose to such a height, that no citizen of superior merit could live in Athens. 'It is the common fault of great and free states, that envy is the concomitant of glory; and that the multitude have a pleasure in humbling all who rise above their own level. The poor can never bear to be spectators of opulence. Chabrias, therefore, absented himself as much as possible from Athens: and not only he, but all the most eminent men did the same, knowing that to be free from envy, they must abandon their country. Thus Conon lived in Cyprus; Iphicrates, in Thrace; Timotheus, in Lesbos; Chabrias, at Sigæum.' – Nepos in Chab: –[154]

Sallust tells us that ingratitude is *a virtue* in a Republic, and that it is reckoned much better to forget a kindness than an injury; to neglect a benefactor, than pardon a criminal. 'In republicá multo præstat beneficii, quam maleficii, immemorem esse. Bonus tantummodo segnior sit, ubi negligas, at malus improbior. Ad hoc, si injuriæ non sint, haud sæpe auxilii egeas.'[155]

It is not uncommon for democratical states to wreak their vengeance on unfortunate, though meritorious commanders: but the Athenians carried this, like every other feature of their republican character, to the most enormous excess, when they executed the six Admirals who had gained the glorious victory of *Arginusæ*; for a neglect, falsely imputed to them, of collecting the bodies of the dead for burial.[156] Some symptoms of the same envious and ungrateful spirit appear in the world, even at this day. In Latin, public odium and envy are expressed by the same word, Invidia.

In Athens as in Rome, the only cure that the popular leaders could devise for these disorders, was a series of ruinous WARS, chiefly with *Republics*. The Peloponessian lasted for twenty six campaigns.[157]

During these wars, the people seemed to change their character. They gloried in being the only people who had erected an *Altar to Mercy*, yet their victories were often stained with almost unexampled avarice and cruelty. They doomed to destruction those *free cities* which had resisted them in a war of iniquitous revenue; and of their operations against aristocratical Republics, we have this summary and memorable account given by Montague – 'Where the Athenians were victors, democracy was settled, or restored; and the people glutted their revenge with the blood of the nobility!'

They themselves fell twice under the despotic power of their own citizens. The first faction was composed of four hundred;[158] the last of thirty; supported by a hostile state, and known by the name of the *Thirty Tyrants*.[159]

As to their internal management, their popular assembly was a scene of faction, clamour, confusion and inconsistency. When it lost the charm of novelty, the attendance of the people was to be obtained only by a pecuniary allowance. By this expedient all the necessitous and profligate were drawn together: the best citizens despised both the company and the temptation. This expedient however was so necessary, that the comic and satirical poet ARISTOPHANES,[160] praising Plutus, the God of riches, asks,

Εκκλησια δ'ουχι δια τουτον γιγνεται;
Is it not he that constitutes our assembly?

Juries were collected by the same mercenary means, and we may guess how they were composed.

At length when public and private virtue was completely undermined; when plays and shews became the occupation of the people; when PHOCION[161] and other master spirits despaired of the national morals; when a band of orators, in the pay of foreign powers, assumed the direction of the people, – they fell at a single blow, under the dominion of PHILIP.[162] By their conduct for several generations after, they shewed that they were as incapable of submitting to slavery, as of enjoying liberty.

Whether *the French* Republic will run the same course, posterity will decide. Whether it has begun it, is a point of which we may judge. Whether or not such a government is preferable to that of England, every one will determine for himself. Whether it is adapted to extensive dominions, has been declared by Montesquieu. 'Il est de la nature d'une Republique, qu'elle n'ait qu'un petit territoire: sans cela elle ne peut guére subsister. Dans un grand Republique, il y a de grandes fortunes, et par consequent peu de moderation dans les esprits: il y a trop grands déspots a mettre entre les mains d'un citoyen.' – It is essential to a republic to have a confined territory. Without this it cannot long exist. In an extensive Republic there must be large properties, consequently little moderation; and the public trusts will be too great to be lodged in the hands of a citizen.[163]

*   *   *

30 October 1793[164]

That the French Statesmen and Philosophers have taken Athens for their model, may be further presumed from their division of time. The Athenian months were divided into decads: the days were named according to their order in each decad: and the last day of the month was also called after Demetrius Poliorcetes,[165] a benefactor of their State. The months took their names from their festivals, in honour of certain remarkable events and celebrated heroes, by which each of them was distinguished. In both countries, time was divided into periods of four years. In both, these periods were denominated olympiads; and as each olympiad among the Greeks was concluded by the olympic games, so the French are to close their olympiads with civic games.

Thoughts on the British Constitution
No. XVII[166]

Aut me amor negotii suscepti fallit, aut nulla unquam Respublica nec major, nec sanctior, nec bonis exemplis ditior fuit.

LIV:[167]

I am either deceived by a partiality for my subject, or there never was a Commonwealth, greater, more venerable, or richer in noble examples.

30 October 1793

The plan of this publication requires several additional papers, but the time of the writers[168] will only admit of a few. The business of these concluding essays shall therefore be to point out two of those subjects which have not yet come under discussion, though of great importance and worthy of a distinct and copious elucidation.

The first is the admirable principles of the COMMON LAW, and the practice of our CRIMINAL JURISPRUDENCE. A just delineation of these subjects would give the inhabitants of this country a much more exalted idea of its constitution than they now entertain, when the generality of them are naturally prone and sedulously taught to dwell on minute blemishes or unavoidable inconveniences: and it would at the same time form a striking contrast with the crudities of modern systems. It could not fail to give an Irishman of humble condition a lively sensation of both pleasure and pride, to compare the process and the evidence necessary to his conviction and punishment, with that which in France decides the fate of a General or a King.[169]

The other point, on which it would be desirable to see a copious publication is this: that the British constitution not only possesses a distinguished advantage in its susceptibility of improvement, but has actually been progressive from the conquest. Though the illustration of this assertion might seem an arduous and even an absurd attempt to the majority of the people, yet to any one conversant with history the fact would be plain and the proof easy. Perhaps it would appear, on such an enquiry, impossible to select a period of fifty years in the history of England, since the constitution assumed a regular form, in which it has not gained additional strength; though possibly no one year could be named, in which the whole people, or a very great proportion of them, did not think it was suffering dilapidation and falling to decay. Nay more, this strange propensity contributes more than any thing else to the stability of that constitution, the ruin of which they are continually deploring. The reason of this discontented temper is, that men are not only more sensible of grievances than of privileges; but an innovation is generally of a more glaring nature, and excites more attention, than an additional security to liberty. An extension of freedom, is no more than their right: a limitation of it, is both an injury and an insult. That this jealousy will tend to secure the inviolability of the beloved object requires no illustration.

Though all the facts that might be adduced to establish this point cannot be brought forward in a paper of this kind, I shall mention a few of them. – By William the Conqueror, who reigned in the latter end of the eleventh century, the Saxon constitution was abolished, the feudal system introduced, and the natives enslaved. Beginning from this period I assert, that the Saxon laws gradually revived, and the constitution gained strength. The

twelfth century opened with the charter of Henry I and was distinguished of that of Stephen, by the constitutions of Clarendon,
by the revival of the laws of Edward the confessor, and by that
signal improvement in liberty and law, the institution of circuits.[170]
The thirteenth century was signalized by Magna Charta, extorted
from John and confirmed by Henry II, by the provisions of Oxford,
the erection of the House of Commons, and the first refusal of
parliament to grant supplies, till grievances were redressed.[171] In
the fourteenth, we find Edward II obliged to grant articles to his
parliament, and parliament denying the power of the King to
grant a subsidy to the Pope. We see the House of Commons taking
its present form by the election of a speaker; and the two estates
first threatening to depose Richard II and afterwards exercising
that great function of the people, the deposition of one King and
the election of another.[172] – In the 15th we meet with that remarkable exercise of parliamentary authority, the appointment of
Protectors during the minority of Henry VI.[173] About the same
time loans began to be obtained on parliamentary security, – and
the House of Commons rose to its natural level by the purchase of
land from the Nobles. The most remarkable extension of liberty in
the sixteenth century, was the abolition of papal authority and
jurisdiction: but notwithstanding the signal abilities and wisdom
of Elizabeth, who reigned for nearly one half of that period, it is
notorious that the House of Commons was gaining and exerting
strength and independence. This was felt in a variety of instances
by her pedantic and pragmatical successor, who was driven to the
most dishonourable expedients to raise the supplies, which parliament refused to grant.[174] Barely to mention the principal instances
of the power of the people in the seventeenth century, would greatly
exceed my limits. Let it suffice to say, that it was distinguished by
the origin of our modern factions, which some think so conducive
to the preservation of liberty. Whigs and Tories were first known

in 1621. The spirit of the people appeared in the Bill of Rights, in the law limiting the duration of parliaments to three years, (1640) in the suppression of the Star-chamber and High Commission Court, the contest about ship money, the prosecution of favourites, the subjection of the clergy to the payment of taxes, and finally, in the war and in the death of the King.[175] – While the same century can boast of many excellent laws obtained by the influence of the people, such as the habeas corpus, the revival of the act for calling triennial parliaments, (1694) which had been repealed under Charles II{,} the act of toleration and the bill of rights;[176] some of the worst that disgrace our statute book originated from the same cause. Thus, the test act and the act of uniformity, were the effect of popular prejudice, and were carried in opposition to the court.[177] We may rank them among the proofs of the fallibility, and of the freedom, of the people. It is scarcely necessary to take notice of those well known and glorious efforts of popular prerogative connected with the Revolution – cashiering and electing their governors, and bestowing the crown in succession. Among the more recent improvements of the eighteenth century, it is sufficient to mention the abolition of feudal jurisdiction, (1745) which extinguished the last remains of hereditary aristocratical tyranny; the independence of the Judges established by William III (13th chap. 2.) and enlarged by his present Majesty, (1st Geo. III 23) – the abolition of general warrants; and the place and pension bill.[178] As a further instance of the progress of the constitution and of our inattention to that progress, I remind the reader of an act which, though not a year old, he has probably forgotten – I mean that law, which ascertained and established two constitutional points of the greatest importance, the right of Juries and the freedom of the Press. The privilege of Jurors to judge of law as well as fact, in case of libels, and consequently the freedom of the Press, are two points that are now become articles of our constitution, and exemplify the manner in which it improves by the perseverance of the people, without revolution, or tumult; not in consequence of a sudden and inconsiderate burst of enthusiasm, but after a deliberate discussion of the subject by the people and parliament. That the right of a Jury to give a verdict upon the whole matter in issue was not established before that act, appears from the necessity of the act itself: and that the freedom of the press was not expressly ascertained by the constitution, is evident from this, that some years ago, no printer dared to report to the people the debates of their Representatives, unless under fictitious names.[179]

In extending this observation to Ireland, I might assert, that as privileges were gained by the English, they were gradually extended to that part of this kingdom which was subject to the King. Thus Henry II granted to his Irish subjects Magna Charta, Charta de Forestis, the Modus tenendi Parliamenta, and the common law of England. Thus in the earliest times we obtained the appointment of Magistrates, and Judges of Assize. Thus were those ancient and salutary laws enacted which secured the people against military and Aristocratical tyranny, and more recently the Habeas Corpus Act, and the independence of the Judges; and thus was the freedom of trade first conferred, and by the liberal explanation of the Navigation Act in the last Session of the British Parliament further extended, by permitting us to supply the markets of Britain with the produce of her own Colonies. I might maintain that in addition to these foreign Auxiliaries we may boast of many securities to liberty, natives of our own soil – the Octennial Bill – the repeal of the Penal Laws – the Emancipation of our Legislature – the restoration of the final judicature – the Irish Libel Bill, and the late act against excessive bail; and I might prove, that for forty years past, few have elapsed without some signal confirmation of freedom. But for the instances, I must refer to the subsequent numbers, and the recollection of those who have inquired into the

History of their Country. – I might appeal to the personal recollection of every man who has paid any attention to what has passed before his eyes since 1778. – But men are so much engrossed by the transactions of the day, that few of them are able and fewer willing, to ascend an eminence and take a comprehensive view of even so short a space.[180] If, however, any man were to extricate himself from the bustle and prejudice of local and temporary politics, and calmly survey that portion of time in which he has been an observer of mankind, he would readily perceive, that this country has improved both in prosperity and liberty. With regard to prosperity, some consider it as a presumptive proof of good Government; while others contend, that we are prosperous in spite of a wretched Constitution and contemptible Governors. Without dwelling on this point which does not admit of demonstration, and on which every man will therefore think as he likes – I shall confine myself to liberty; for here I am in no danger of contradiction, the facts being numerous, striking and notorious.

Nor do I hold out *this* country as an exception to the general state of THE WORLD, as if liberty were flourishing here, while she was expiring in every other part of Europe. Were I to do so, I might justly be suspected of partiality. I consider Ireland as only one instance of an undeniable fact – that the human race, considered as one great community, is progressive in knowledge, liberality, prosperity and liberty. Nay, I do not hesitate to say, that they have made greater advances in these important interests within the last thirty years, than in any former period of equal length. If therefore, my contending that Ireland was an exception to the general condition of mankind would have been a presumption of partiality, may I not suspect him of some undue bias, who maintains that its condition is an exception to the general improvement of the world?

But many who will readily admit that the condition of their country has been meliorated in every other period of its History, will except the present era; and few of our more active patriots can patiently hear it asserted, that at this day the kingdom is making advances in liberty. Yet even this I think probable from reason, and certain from fact. I will even restrict my assertion to that point of time in which liberty has received the severest wounds, and maintain, that on striking the balance of the last Session, the result will be found favourable to freedom. From the concluding numbers, every man will be able to judge for himself. Without anticipating what will there be stated, I shall only submit some observations, which I wish him to keep in mind.

The first is, that if the Constitution had received damage it is to be ascribed rather to the folly and precipitation of an infatuated faction, than to the power of Administration, however well inclined to encroach upon it. While it was vilifying by faction, and undermining by men in power, the enlightened friends of their country lamented in silence and inaction, their follies and their crimes.

This is intimately connected with the second truth, that even the most censurable acts of the last session were passed with the approbation or acquiescence of the most strenuous friends of the people in Parliament; of a great majority of men of property, education, and abilities, out of doors; and even of a large proportion of the subjects in inferior ranks.[181] Much as these acts are condemned *now*, not a single petition appeared against them at the time. Whether this consent was obtained by the artifice of the castle in deluding the nation, or by the desperate folly of a party who terrified their countrymen, it is plain that what was effected with the concurrence of so great a portion of the community cannot be strong evidence of the decay of the Constitution. I rather conclude, that every thing we gained is to be attributed to the influence of the people and the vigour of that Constitution; while every thing we have lost was given up in a panic, in order to secure the peaceable enjoyment of the remainder. At least this seemed to be the general impression. If the people were deceived, there is no form of government under which they are less exposed to deception; and whether deceived or not, the general consent of the wealth, information, and talents of the country, would even under a well ordered government be taken for the sense of the people. The Gun-powder and Convention Bills, the augmentation of the army, and the extension of the privileges of the Lords, were like the appointment of a Dictator.[182] But it should be remembered, that the power of the Roman Dictator continued but six months, and that it was generally resigned before that period. If Government have not moderation to give up the dictatorial authority with which they are invested as soon as the danger is past, I have no doubt, that their lictors will be dismissed, and their fasces broken, by the constitutional efforts of the nation.

In the third place, as we uniformly find both from history and the experience of our own times, that every good and necessary plan, when long persisted in by the people, has been carried; so every unconstitutional innovation has either become obsolete or been expressly abolished: and while the Place and Pension Acts, the reduction and limitation of the pension List, and the act declaratory of the Rights of Juries, will be enrolled within our indefeasible privileges, the obnoxious measures of that session will be classed with the ancient claims of Britain to make laws and administer justice for Ireland. Through the vigilance of the people, those acts which are not sanctioned by the constitution, may be removed in time; while the abrogation of the good ones which accompanied them as *palliatives*, can with an ill grace be repealed by the most abandoned government.

Lastly, waving these considerations, I might put the question upon the simple issue of a fair balance struck between the measures even of that unpopular session. I might state the acts first enumerated – against the Secret Committee, the Gun-powder Act, and the Delegation Act.[183]

Thoughts on the British Constitution
No. XVIII[184]

Dans l'Aristocratie, la Souveraine Puissance est entre les mains
d'un certain nombre de personnes. Ce sont elles qui font les Loix
& qui les font executer, & le reste du peuple n'est tout au–plus á leur
égard, que comme dans une Monarchie les sujets sont a l'égard du
Monarque.

In an Aristocracy the Supreme Power is in the hands of a certain
number of individuals, who make and execute their laws. The rest
of the people are their subjects.

L'ESPRIT DES LOIX

{*No date*}

The aristocratical governments of some continental Republics,
are justly reprobated. The privileges of the Nobles in France were
so highly oppressive, as in a great measure to cause and justify the
Revolution. In the course of the struggle, the term 'Aristocrate'
has been applied to every friend of order and subordination, who
has opposed the anarchical extravagancies of the most contemptible demagogues: and unhappily this style of speaking has been
introduced into this country to corrupt both our language and our
principles. Every man that differs from certain popular writers,
is denominated an aristocrate; and I have no doubt, that some
expressions in the preceding essay will procure me the honour of

the same appellation. In vindication therefore of the constitution and myself, I deny that there is any *establishment* in this country which deserves the title of aristocracy, in an invidious sense. A government entirely exercised by Nobles, is justly reprobated as the worst of all tyrannies; and even where the administration of a kingly government is exclusively conducted by them, they add to the oppressive nature of absolute power, and defeat the intentions of a limited monarchy: nay if they form a cast, so that their cabals cannot be disconcerted, or their pride checked by the admission of commoners into their number, I freely confess, that such an order is a diseased and deformed member of the political body. But such an order does not exist in Great Britain or Ireland. The Lords are neither the rulers nor ministers of the country: they can neither make nor execute laws of themselves: their families and relations are commoners: and they are continually obliged to receive persons even of mean origin, but splendid abilities, knowledge, or merit, into their house.

Take a view of the actual distribution of power in these countries. In England the most efficient offices of the state are necessarily held by members of the House of Commons: the highest posts in the law are always held by commoners or newly created peers: and the dignities of the church are generally in the hands of men of low birth; their honours dying with them, whatever attachment they feel to the crown, they are slenderly connected with the coronet. The great officers in the army and navy are, with few exceptions, of the same description. But the most striking proof of this point is a fact which is within the knowledge of all my readers. Cast your eye over the distribution of power in *this* kingdom. It is entirely in the hands of men of humble origin, excepting the viceroy. Who are the men that administer the affairs of this country? Are the Lord High Chancellor, the Lord Primate, and the Archbishops men of noble birth? No. Yet these men take precedence of all the nobility. The

Secretary of State, the Chancellor of the Exchequer, the Attorney and Solicitor General, in short all the men who transact the business of government in the House of Commons, are necessarily commoners. If any of the judges are ennobled, it is only in consequence of their promotion, that they may assist in the deliberations in the supreme court of judicature. Who are the men, that are rapidly advancing to these situations? Many of them persons of no patrimony or pedigree. There is a family of commoners in this kingdom which eclipses the majority of the lords, as much in wealth and influence, as in princely munificence. I speak it to their praise when I say, that they are men of low origin, of no pedigree in *this* country, and even now engaged in commercial business.[185] I speak it to the praise of the constitution, when I add, that were it not invidious, I could shew that all the exalted personages above mentioned are *novi homines*,[186] men that in the best days of the Roman Republic would not have been suffered to aspire to the lowest offices of the state, or to a seat in the senate. The whole power of the monarch, in both countries, is always wielded and sometimes controlled by men on a level as to title or privilege, with the meanest of the people. There is no obstacle to any man of talents. The administration of the empire is within his grasp.

I can never consent to call that an aristocratical government, in which private gentlemen like C. J. Fox, the present minister, and his illustrious father, direct the whole machine of the state, and influence or even dictate the politics of Europe; and in which I see Dukes, Marquisses and Earls, performing menial offices about the person, household, or stable of the King. Nor can I, on the other hand, suspect that this reverse of condition proceeds from the despotism of the Monarch; since in the course of my life, every change in the King's councils has been dictated by the people, often in opposition to the wishes of his Majesty.

There are some people, though, it is to be hoped, few in this country, that consider *the rich* as an aristocracy; that hold in suspicion every man who has a whole suit of clothes; that think every independent man an enemy of liberty; every opulent man a tyrant; and who by branding all kind of subordination with the name of slavery, all influence with that of tyranny, would treat men of property or authority as Tarquin treated the poppies in his garden.[187] But the result of such crude extravagancies will always be the effect which that tyrant thus depictured. When a state abounds with persons of influence and wealth, it will not be easy even for a King to usurp absolute power. When all are equal, the first man or party that can rise above the level by wealth, or eloquence, or courage, or cunning, or any other means, becomes the lord of all.

With these atrocious follies I must be excused from arguing.

While I thus deny the existence of any *privileged order*, which deserves the name of ARISTOCRACY in the invidious sense of the word, I am far from wishing to defend our numerous corrupt and depopulated boroughs, or that unconstitutional influence which men of property often exert at elections. These have already been the subject of pointed reprobation in former numbers of this publication. But these are only defects in the democratical part of the constitution; for this influence is neither confined to the nobles, nor is it necessarily hereditary. It may be possessed by any man who can acquire property, and is subject to fluctuation and transfer; being at one time connected with a title of nobility; presently, attached to the landed estate of a commoner; and soon after in the hands of an opulent merchant.

Many schemes have been devised for correcting the inequality and the influence of property: but all that I have seen are pregnant with greater evils than they pretend to extirpate, and threaten to rob men of dearer privileges than they affect to secure. To those who adopt these notions, every superior is an aristocrate, and men can never be free, while they have any rights remaining; for an inequality property must necessarily subsist, till men shall be deprived of the privileges which they hold most dear, such as disposing of their fortunes and governing their families. A late paradoxical and visionary tract on political justice (Godwin's Political Justice, Vol. ii. p. 381–384. Dublin Edition.) has carried the notions which have been controverted in these papers, to such a ludicrous excess, that one might well suspect it to be a piece of refined satire, conducted with the gravest irony. The author having laid it down as a maxim, that men have no rights, proceeds to recommend a state of society, if it can be so called, in which they will be subject to no government. This he calls a system of 'individuality.' Lest any two persons should unite, he abolishes marriage, and establishes in its room a promiscuous intercourse of the sexes; and lest this should produce too powerful an effect, he speaks of a subsequent period at which ALL intercourse between them is to be renounced; and men are by virtue of his plan to become IMMORTAL upon earth, (Godwin, Vol. ii, p. 393.)[188] – But what connects these remarks with his present subjects is his whimsical idea of aristocracy. For any man to have a wife, he pronounces to be a violation of equality; to wish to know his own children is an unpardonable instance of family pride; and it would be quite inconsistent with the system of 'individuality' to assume that insolent and oppressive mark of distinction, a surname. By reprobating every form of government that has ever been attempted or devised, and holding out this as the only alternative, he contrives to leave his readers in very good humour with their present lot, and ready to exclaim –

– Rather bear those ills we have,
Than fly to others that we know not of.

Shall we then, with the presumption of a modern theorist, consider our constitution as perfect; or like a satellite of despotism, maintain that this is a time at which reformation should be postponed? A patriot of the old stamp will rather say – the constitution has received improvement in every situation of affairs, in peace and in war, by its native vigour, and by the exertions of the people. It is always progressive, or retrograde; never at rest: seeming to decline for a time, but often, like Anteus, deriving strength from its falls; and, like the Hydra, life from its wounds.[189] Let the people retain their jealousy and their constancy; their jealousy will protect it from violation, their constancy will guard them against meretricious arts of a more youthful mistress; but let them not be deluded by pretences, that ANY TIME is unfit for a reform upon constitutional principles.

Nothing has been farther from my intention in the course of these papers, than to present a picture of our government under false or flattering colours. To give a just one, and to vindicate the many excellent qualities of the original, was my single aim. Whether it deserves the character I have drawn, may be tried by the following axiom – that THERE IS NOT A REAL GRIEVANCE OF WHICH THE PEOPLE COMPLAIN WHICH THAT VERY CONSTITUTION, IF IN FULL OPERATION, WOULD NOT REMOVE. To establish this position, there is little more to be done than refer to the seventh number of these THOUGHTS, where some of its fundamental principles are enumerated, and their legal foundations pointed out. By that touchstone let the most obnoxious acts of any session be tried, and if their principles be not there disclaimed, every portion of my defence may fall to the ground.

Is it our complaint, that juries may be unfairly impannelled? – By ancient usage the sheriffs were elective.

Do special juries intrench upon the liberty of the subject? – They are novelties of a modern date.

Can the subject be fined or imprisoned to any amount and for an indefinite term, without trial by his peers, without being confronted with his accuser? – Magna charta expressly opposes it.

A moment's recollection will convince us that every unconstitutional point which is brought to this test, will meet the state of those adduced. If then the PRINCIPLES of British freedom come from this ordeal with untainted honor, and every deviation in PRACTICE can be traced back to the people who have suffered it – who is to blame – the constitution, or themselves? If ever there was a form of government calculated to administer itself for ages, and to preserve an undiminished lustre without the intervention and jealous care of the collective body, let the British one stand accountable for every blemish. But if none such ever did exist, our system of civil policy is as little chargeable with its present abuses, as any other of which either the ancient or modern world furnishes examples.

The constitution is a goodly fabric, the foundations of which are still solid and entire. Some of its buttresses have been suffered through the negligence of the owners, to fall into decay. These have only to be repaired, that it may answer every purpose of its erection. If I am asked, how is this to be effected? – by union, and a determined spirit among the people.

Were we not divided among ourselves, and too apt to wander from the object, a reform might experience a temporary resistance, but the struggle would peaceably terminate in success. However problematical it may appear, a deranged republic would have greater difficulties to encounter, in a restoration to its primitive principles, than that form of government which is admired in proportion as it is minutely examined, and is most censured where least understood.

Nothing in this world is stationary, but all subject to change. Those institutions, therefore, which make allowance for the progressive declension of states from the highest eminence of virtue,

are best calculated for imperfect beings. An author who has been a
standard with former generations, and whose works will survive
the wrecks of modern politics, informs us in the motto of the
second number – that –

> To produce *great political good*, less virtue is required in A MONARCHY,
> than in any other form of Government.'
>
> MONTESQUIEU

Thoughts on the British Constitution
No. XIX[190]

It will be found, if I mistake not, a true observation in Politics, that the two extremes in Government, *liberty and slavery*, commonly approach nearest to each other; and that, as you depart from the extremes, and mix a little of monarchy with liberty, the Government becomes always the more free.

HUME[191]

7 November 1793

The following is offered as a brief and imperfect sketch of some of the most remarkable parts in the History of the Constitution of Ireland.

Anno 1494. From the 10th of Henry VII a parliament could not be summoned in Ireland, till the articles proposed to be passed in it were previously certified to the King, and after his Majesty in his English Council had *considered* and *approved*, or *altered* said act intended to be passed, then and not sooner could a parliament be holden; but no other acts than those so certified could be introduced.

[From the 3d and 4th of William and Mary, it was allowed that *new* causes might be certified, after the session had actually commenced.]

From the enacting of Poyning's law, 10th Henry VII all statutes that had passed in England were to be of force in Ireland, and subsequent ones, in which Ireland was included, were considered as in force there.[192]

[This was necessarily extended in 1782 (by Mr Yelverton's bill) to subsequent acts; for the quiet and settlement of possessions held in Ireland, under no other titles.][193]

It was the usage of parliament until of very late years, that Irish laws were brought in as *heads of bills*, and presented to the Lord Lieutenant for the time being, who might, or might not, as he and the council thought proper, transmit them for the King's consideration.

Of course between the privy councils of the two kingdoms, parliament was rendered a nullity, and their deliberations a name.

Anno 1698. 'Molyneux's case of Ireland being bound by acts of parliament in England,' was burned by the hands of the common hangman of London, after the house of commons of Great Britain had voted that unanswerable book, (the principles of which are now the law of our land) to be 'of dangerous consequence to the crown and people of Ireland,' and addressed the King on its pernicious tendencies.[194]

The King could assure his Commons in one of the countries which he governed (England), that his Majesty would do all that in him lay to discourage the *woollen* trade in his other kingdom (Ireland). A compromise, however, was graciously made that the *linen* trade should be left entirely to us. And such was the baneful influence of a British court at that day, that while an Irish parliament passed an act laying heavy duties on the exports of woollens of its own country to *England*, the English parliament in the succeeding year even prohibited Irish export *to other countries*; so that between the parliament of the one country and the other, the manufacture bade fair for total annihilation.

Anno 1719. In an appeal from the Irish court of exchequer to the Irish Lords, the decree of exchequer was reversed. The person whose property was affected by the reversal, made an appeal from

his own country to the *British Lords*, who acting on the principle
that an *Irish* House of Lords possessed no judicial powers, confirmed the first decree, in opposition to the reversal of the Irish
Lords; and the Barons from the exchequer of Ireland were actually
obliged to restore possession of the estates in litigation, according
to the English reversal.[195]

On the other hand, the lady who was injured by the reversal of
the Irish Lords decree, petitioned their house; in consequence of
which the Barons of the Irish exchequer were taken into custody
for acting under *an order of the British House*; and a representation
of the case was forthwith transmitted to the King. This representation being laid by him before his British Lords, they beseeched
his Majesty to confer some act of Royal favour on the Barons of
the Irish exchequer for their conduct on the occasion, and framed
a bill which passed into a law, denying all right in the Lords of
Ireland to exercise any judicial power, to judge of, affirm, or reverse,
any judgment, or decree, given even in any of the courts of their
own country; assuming that, as an exclusive privilege of their own,
which was denied to *our* Lords, in affairs merely affecting ourselves.

Anno 1720. 6 Geo. I. The right of Great Britain to bind Ireland
by acts of her legislature, having been called in question, – the
British Parliament passed an act declaratory of what was the law of
England on that point, viz. That 'the kingdom of Ireland *ought to
be subordinate to and dependant* upon the imperial crown of Great
Britain, as being inseparably annexed and united thereto; and that
the King's Majesty, with the consent of the Lords and Commons
of Great Britain in parliament assembled, hath powers to make
laws for Ireland.'[196]

At this time Roman Catholics could hold leases only for 31
years; our trade was intolerably shackled; and our Parliaments
were unlimited in their duration, unless the King pleased to dis-
solve them, or they suffered dissolution by his death.

It is now time to look at the reverse of the picture, which will convince any man that every thing may be obtained by *perseverance*; as the difficulties which our ancestors had to cope with, sunk under their steady unremitting endeavours.

Anno 1723. Woods half pence. Dean Swift, seized that occasion slyly to raise a spirit of enquiry into the rights of Ireland as an independent kingdom. The English government taking advantage of a scarcity of copper coin in this country, granted a patent to Mr. Woods for fourteen years, to be an exclusive coiner of half pence and farthings for Ireland, to the amount of 108,000*l.* His coin was base, and the whole a gross imposition; but the spirit of the country under its great leader prevailed. One of the first acts of Lord Carteret, as Lord Lieutenant, was a proclamation offering 300*l.* reward for discovering the author of the *Draper's fourth Letter*, in which Irish rights were proclaimed by the Dean, under that fictitious title.[197]

Anno 1753. – Previous consent. A contest with the crown, whether a surplus of revenue then remaining in the Irish treasury, after all the public burthens had been discharged, was at the disposal of parliament for public purposes; or at the will of the crown, to be taken out of the treasury by a King's letter. The question at first was, whether royal consent was necessary, before parliament could apply this unappropriated sum toward the discharge of the national debt. Parliament denied that it was:– but his Majesty, after a considerable time, settled the point, by taking it out of the treasury by his own letter. The crown triumphed; but the people were taught to think; to enquire into their rights; and to combine their force by means of popular clubs, in order to assert and recover them.[198]

Even subsequent to this period, such a veil was drawn between the collective body and their representatives, that the PRESS, now a dreaded engine of popular power, dare not publish debates without exhibiting the speakers, whether courtiers or patriots, under fictitious names; – ransacking the annals of Greece and Rome for names to cover those really intended.

Anno 1764. – GENERAL WARRANTS had been in practice even from the Revolution, without having ever been called in question; till the committal of John Wilkes to the Tower, as the author of Number forty-five of the North Briton, brought the legality of them into question, and ended in their virtual abolition in England, and of course in Ireland, to the great improvement of the consti-tution.[199] Of this, a slight enquiry into their nature will afford sufficient proof. These warrants had been issued by Secretaries of State; and they were termed *general*, because it was not necessary that they should even contain the names of the particular persons charged with the offence. They went to authorize any number of men, however mean and contemptible, to apprehend and seize the reputed authors, printers, and publishers of any writing which Secretaries of State chose to deem seditious. The most innocent man might be dragged from his bed, and hurried to a prison; his papers rummaged, and those of the utmost value to himself or his family, though the public were no way concerned in them, might be concealed, or destroyed; and secrets of the utmost delicacy and of the most private nature, revealed. Thus a highly dangerous discretionary power was exercised over the liberty of the subject, not by magistrates only, but by the most profligate of mankind, the inferior officers of justice; and all this in the mere case of a *supposed libel*, before proof was brought to a jury that it was any libel, or that the accused was author, printer, or publisher of the paper in question. How this power might have been and was abused, by an improper minister, and how indefensible it was on every principle of the constitution, it is unnecessary to point out.

Anno 1768. A bill was carried for limiting the duration of Irish parliaments to seven years, as in England; it was returned, altered to *eight* years in the British Privy Council; and so altered, it passed and continues in force.[200]

Anno 1778. The encreased spirit of the nation produced the Volunteer Association, the admirable effects of which need not here be enumerated.[201]

Roman Catholics in Ireland were empowered by law to take leases for any term of years not exceeding 999, or for any term determinable on any number of lives not exceeding five; in place of thirty-one years, which was the longest term they could enjoy before that time.[202]

Anno 1779. The encreased influence of the people on the conduct of parliament, produced *a six-months money bill*, as means of extorting a free trade from Great Britain. In the December of that year, the Minister carried a repeal of the British law which had prohibited the exportation of Irish manufactures made of, or mixed with wool, from any part of Ireland; also the repeal of a law prohibiting the exportation of glass into Ireland that was not of British manufacture, and prohibiting the exportation of it from this country to others.

Ireland was at the same time permitted to export and import commodities to and from the British Colonies in America, and the West Indies, and the British settlements on the coast of Africa.[203]

Anno 1780. Mr. Grattan in the Irish House of Commons moved, that 'no power on earth, save the King, Lords and Commons of Ireland, have a right to make laws to bind this country.' – *Motion lost!*

Parliament having passed a limited mutiny bill, for legalizing the existence of an army from session to session, it was returned from England with an unconstitutional alteration rendering it *perpetual*.

A modification of Poyning's law was rejected, and a bill for establishing the independence of the judges met the same fate.

Anno 1781. The same salutary bills were again brought forward, and treated with similar contempt.

Notwithstanding this, in the very year following,

Anno 1782. The *declaratory* law of England, 6 Geo. I asserting a right to legislate for this country, which had long and deservedly been so obnoxious to us; was repealed by the British parliament. And now the influence of the people of Ireland *out of* parliament was strongly marked; for, after the whole point of legislation seemed to be settled between the two countries, respecting the dereliction of the British claim to make laws for Ireland, and of her Lords to act as a court of dernier appeal, new discontents arose among us, to which England had to submit by a law of the 26th of his present Majesty, expressly renouncing the pretended right, in the following terms. 'The said right claimed by the people of Ireland, to be bound only by laws enacted by his Majesty and the parliament of that kingdom, in *all cases whatsoever*, and to have all actions and suits of law or in equity, which may be instituted in that kingdom, decided in his Majesty's courts therein, finally and without appeal from thence, shall be and it is hereby declared to be established and ascertained for ever, and shall at no time thereafter be questioned or questionable.'

All the injurious restrictions of the law of Poyning's, that had for two hundred and eighty-eight years sapped the vital principle of debate, and of a free parliament, were done away.[204]

A Mutiny Bill for legalizing the existence of the army, limiting its duration to two years, and subjecting it to the controul of our own parliament instead of the British one, was carried into a law. On a former occasion when an Irish act had passed, taking some trifling cognizance of the army on our establishment, the late Lord Chatham taxed the English Minister with having thus 'suffered the strongest quill to be plucked from the eagle's wing.'

A Habeas Corpus law was also passed, which Ireland never before enjoyed, though England had.

Roman Catholics were enabled to purchase or possess lands by grant, limitation, descent or devise; to dispose of them by will descendable according to the course of common law, devisable and transferable as the lands of Protestants.[205]

Several penal acts were repealed, viz. those against the hearing and celebrating of mass; against a Roman Catholic having a horse of or above the value of five pounds; as well as those which empowered grand juries to levy from them the amount of any losses sustained by privateers, required them to provide watchmen, and totally excluded them as inhabitants of the city of Limerick or its suburbs. They were no longer prohibited from keeping schools *publicly*, or teaching persons of their own profession *privately*; and the guardianship of their children was restored to the parents.[206]

By ancient usage the judges held their offices during the King's pleasure, and lost them at his death, in order that his successor might have the nomination of his own judges. The bad effects of this corrupt connexion between the crown and the bench were often written in letters of blood. By an English statute of William III their commissions were made to continue during their own *good behaviour*, instead of the *King's pleasure*, and their salaries fixed; at the same time that they were removable by the King on the joint address of both houses of parliament.

His present Majesty, among other salutary improvements, opened his reign with recommending that it should be enacted (which it accordingly was) that even the demise of the King should not put an end to the commission of the Judges; but that they should continue without intermission as if no such event had taken place, and continue to have the salaries allowed them by law. This excellent improvement on the constitution, which was enjoyed by our sister country from the accession of his Majesty George III was not granted to Ireland for twenty-two years afterwards, to wit, till a few months after the first Dungannon meeting had pointed out, in a very spirited resolution, the necessity for the judges being rendered as independent in this kingdom as in Great Britain.[207]

Anno 1785. A place and pension bill, proposed by Mr Forbes, was rejected.[208]

Great Britain tried her strength as far as prudence would permit, in favour of a certain commercial adjustment with Ireland, in which some obnoxious clauses were introduced. The minister carried it by a majority of nineteen in our House of Commons (127 to 108); but was obliged to withdraw the bill, because the sense of *the people was against it.*[209]

Anno 1788. A bill brought in to reduce the interest of money in Ireland from six to five per cent as in England, it passed the Commons, but was thrown out in the Lords. [An instance of the use of two deliberative houses.]

Anno 1789. The printer of a newspaper in Dublin had published certain libels on some obscure characters. The Chief Justice, at the instance and on the affidavits of the aggrieved, issued his FIATS, to hold the printer to special bail in the sum of seven thousand eight hundred pounds. – The action being a common one of slander, and the damages accruing to the complainants uncertain, it was alleged that holding the printer to special bail at all, was inadmissible and only allowable in actions of scandalum magnatum, or of slander of title. The printer was however thrown into jail. His council shortly after moved to dismiss him on common bail, or no bail at all, which he proved to be consistent with law, and conformable to the uniform practice of the British courts; tho' it was to be confessed that there were many instances in Ireland in favour of the judge. Over ruled by the court in that point, the lawyer shewed from the uncertain nature of the injuries incurred, and the low situations of the parties aggrieved, that the bail demanded was excessive, and should be diminished. The affidavit of the printer was likewise produced, stating that 'in consequence of frequent and vexatious arrests, by fiats and otherwise, and by libellous publications,' he was so injured in his credit as to be unable to find bail for more than five hundred pounds. The motion was refused, and the person accused remanded to Newgate. This transaction occasioned great agitations. Cases were imagined in which a patriot might fall under the displeasure of a corrupt administration, and by means of an affidavit sworn against him by any unprincipled wretch, stating damages to such an amount as he could not find bail for, fiats might issue at the discretion of a judge; he might be thrown into a jail, and there remain three terms before he could enter a *non-pros*. Being at that period discharged, he has no remedy for his loss of liberty, but in following the plaintiff. The plaintiff is a man of straw, and has fled. This case brought itself home to the feelings of every one, and we deemed ourselves undone. Mark the consequence. As the oppression of an individual gave birth to the *Habeas Corpus* act of 31 Carolus II so the printer, in the case now mentioned, suffered grievously, but the very severity of his case, produced an excellent law, which passed in the 31st of his present Majesty. To prevent vexatious arrests and proceedings in actions of slander, the WRIT or process, can no longer be marked for a greater sum than *two hundred* pounds, in any case in which *actual* damages are not set forth and sworn to; and no defendant in such action can be held to SPECIAL bail in a greater sum than two hundred pounds, except where actual damages are set forth and sworn to by plaintiff; and where actual damages are so sworn to, the court or judge may at discretion admit defendant to bail, in a lesser sum than the amount of the damages sworn to.

Thoughts on the British Constitution
No. XX[210]

This is a season of virtue, and public spirit. Let us take advantage of it to repeal those laws which infringe our liberties, and introduce such as may restore the vigour of our ancient constitution.

SIR JOHN ST AUBIN[211]

(SUBJECT OF THE LAST NUMBER RESUMED AND CONCLUDED)

7 November 1793

Anno 1793. The session of this year opened with an admission of the principle, that A REFORM IN THE REPRESENTATION demanded the serious attention of the Legislature. On the fourteenth of January, the servants of the crown and the commons at large, consented that that grand desideratum should be investigated in a committee of the whole house, on the 12th of the following month. As it is seldom considered the interest of assemblies to abridge their own power, or hold out any hope of it to the people, nothing but popular influence, through whatever channels, or upon whatever passions it operated, could have produced this effect. The twelfth of February arrived. Mr Grattan's preparatory motions were lost by the question of adjournment, and the subject was not resumed during the session.[212] Had the kingdom come forward before that decision, success seemed inevitable; but it remained silent, because intimidated; and at the very moment when a reform seemed attainable, it fell to the ground. If the favourable reception which it met with be attributed to the violence of a party, in the first instance; the intimidation of the people at large was the result of that violence, in the second; and the loss of the cause, in the third.

Such are the natural consequences of threats without power; of advancing extravagant lengths, when the people neither follow nor approve; of slighting the constitution, and threatening it as a non-entity, at the very crisis when an adherence to its principles is wise as well as politic, because it affords the best prospect of union and success.[213]

The necessity of a reform, as forcibly stated by Mr Grattan, deserves to be recorded. He asserted, and no man denied, that of the three hundred members of which our representative house consists, two hundred are returned by individuals, instead of bodies of electors. From forty to fifty are returned by ten persons. Of the three hundred; the counties, counties of cities and towns, and university, return eighty-four, leaving two hundred and fifteen for the boroughs and manors. Several of those boroughs have no resident elector at all, some of them but one; and on the whole, two thirds of the representatives are returned by less than one hundred persons. The defence of such a state of things, on the plea of ANTIQUITY, he deemed absurd. So far from its being derived from antient times, from the Saxons, the age of the Confessor, or after the English intercourse with Ireland, at the time of King John, or the reign of Edward; James the First! was the King who made forty boroughs to return eighty members. In 1613, the numbers returned to parliament were two hundred and thirty-two. Since that time sixty-eight members have been added, ALL by the house of STUART; one by Anne, four by James the Second, most of the remainder by Charles the First, with a view to religious distinctions, and by

Charles the Second, with a view to personal favour. The form of the constitution was twelve COUNTIES, established in the reign of King John. Henry the Eighth added one; Mary two; and Elizabeth seventeen. Since that æra the counties have received no additions whatever; though between the year 1613 and the present, the borough interest has received an addition of sixty-eight members, which is more than the whole county representation. He estimated the property of each of the one hundred individuals, or constituents, who return two hundred members, at four thousand pounds per annum, on an average; of course all the property they represented did not exceed 400,000*l*. – though, says he, they vote through their representatives, near two millions in taxes. In other words, there are two thirds of the house, voting near two millions of money every year, and not representing half a million. In this forcible point of view he placed our present establishment with respect to the representation of PROPERTY. His other arguments were equally unanswerable.

In England, for many years, Officers of the Revenue have been disqualified from *voting* at elections. The acceptance of any office created *before* 1705 vacates the seat of the member, and sends him back to his constituents for re-election or otherwise. The acceptance of an office created there *since* 1705, vacates the seat and renders the possessor totally ineligible.

PLACE AND PENSION BILL – In Ireland, by an act of last sessions (33d year of his present Majesty), no person can hereafter be elected a member of parliament, who shall hold a new place of profit, created after that act, nor any one who holds a pension for years, or during pleasure, or whose wife shall hold one. Neither can surveyors general, nor collectors of revenue, whether customs or excise, (except in Dublin) nor secretaries to the commissioners of customs and excise, to the commissioners of accounts, to the commissioners of barracks, to the post office, or to the board of ordnance; nor paymaster of corn bounties coast ways, be hereafter members. Every office revived after five years disuse, or where more than one hundred pounds a year is added to the salary; – or where one hundred pounds a year shall be granted to any office to which no salary is now annexed, – shall be deemed a new office, and consequently disqualify the person who holds it from sitting. If a member of parliament after 31st December 1793, accepts an office of profit, he vacates his seat; but is capable of re-election. The number of commissioners for the execution of any office, is limited to what was usual at or before the first day of the present parliament. Officers in the Army, Militia and Navy, may be elected as heretofore, also persons having or accepting an office for life or during good behaviour. And an oath in future is to be taken by every member, that he does not hold in his own name, or in the name of any person in trust for him, any PENSION, for years or during his Majesty's pleasure, or any OFFICE OR PLACE which is rendered by the act of parliament incompatible with his holding a seat in the house of commons.[214]

Tho' these provisions fall short of what we should require, no one can deny that they are valuable accessions. They deprive the present and future governments of a power which they formerly exercised, of creating new places to strengthen their interest in parliament;* at the same time that they prevent pensioners for years or during pleasure from ever hereafter becoming members,† and they cut off a train of Surveyors General, Collectors of the Revenue (of Excise and Customs) Commissioners of Accounts,

---

* The reader will perceive the value of this restriction, when he recollects that from 1769 to 1789, forty new parliamentary places had arisen, fourteen of which had been created in the course of six months of the latter year. In that year, on some great popular question, the minister mustered a majority of one hundred and forty-four – one hundred and four of which were placemen and pensioners! Who, considering these things, can with a safe conscience say a reform is unnecessary?

† In five years prior to 1790, pensions were granted to eleven members of parliament, to the wives of others, and to four or five peers of the realm.

&c. several of whom now vote in the house. And any member accepting an office of profit (unless he holds it for life or during good behaviour) vacates his seat, but is not disqualified from being again returned if his constituents deem him eligible.*

In the same session, was passed that admirable bill which had shortly before been introduced by Mr. Fox into the British House of Commons, where it is also law, declaring the right of Juries, in the case of libels. It enables them 'to give verdict on the whole matter in issue;' of course renders them judges both of law and fact. The reader will recollect the strenuous opposition given to this principle by Lord Mansfield, and Lord Camden's long and consistent support of it; and he will perceive in its success what hopes may be entertained of any measure founded on reason, and pursued with ardour.[215]

In same session, we had an act for granting a civil list establishment in lieu of the hereditary revenue, which formerly arose from certain duties and taxes. The pensions paid out of that list amounted in 1789 to the enormous sum of 108,280*l.* In order to reduce it to 80,000*l.* (the sum formerly proposed by the patriots and rejected) the act declares that from the twenty-fifth March, 1794, the pensions granted in any one year shall not exceed 1,200*l.* until the list be thereby reduced to 80,000*l.* And after it is so reduced, no pension can be granted for the use of any one person, of a sum exceeding 1,200*l.* except to the Royal Family, or on an address of either house of parliament. Secret service money is limited to 5,000*l.* except for preventing or detecting conspiracies; and

---

* In England, with respect to ELECTION, revenue officers cannot vote for members in parliament, by which means a great number of trained veterans in the sale of public trusts, are cut off from the elective body; – an improvement which ought to be made in our own country, and which its patriots should strenuously insist on. – The British bill for disqualifying revenue officers was introduced in the year 1770, but scouted. It was revived by a Mr. Crewe, from whence it has been called Crewe's bill; and after it had been repeatedly presented and as often dismissed, it passed both houses of parliament in 1782, and received the Royal sanction when Charles Fox came into administration.

concordatum limited to the same sum, or thirty pounds a year to any one person.

In the same session, an act passed *to encourage the improvement of barren land*, such as barren heath and waste ground. Lands of this description, which have paid no tythes, and which hereafter shall be improved and converted into arable ground or meadow, are henceforth for seven years next after the time of improving the same, to be exempted from the payment of tythes. Such was the dread of touching, or in any manner interfering with whatever concerned the church, that an outcry was formerly raised against every idea of exempting from tythe (when they should be rendered of any value) lands which did not even pay it formerly.[216]

In the same session, the act for the relief of his Majesty's Roman Catholic subjects of Ireland, carries internal evidence that the voice of the people, or of a majority of them, cannot long be raised in vain, though opposed by men the highest in office and in power. Roman Catholics are restored to the elective franchize; but they are required previously to election to have taken in the Four Courts, or at the Quarter Sessions, an oath of allegiance, (passed in the thirteenth and fourteenth year of the present reign) and made a declaration upon oath with regard to certain points of faith connected with morals; such as detesting the principle of its being lawful to murder, destroy, or injure any person under pretence of being a heretic; doing any thing that is wrong, for the good of the church, or in obedience to any ecclesiastical power whatever; declaring that it is not an article of the catholic faith that the Pope is infallible; and that he who makes the declaration does not believe that at the will of a Pope sins can be forgiven; and that he will defend the arrangement of property in this country as established by the laws now in being; and he abjures any intention to subvert the present church establishment. They are not allowed to vote at parish vestries, or to carry arms, unless seized of a freehold estate of 100*l.* a year, or possessed of a personal estate of 1,000*l.* or upwards; nor unless possessing a freehold estate of 10*l.* yearly value and less than 100*l.* or a personal estate of 300*l.* and less than 1,000*l.* having taken the oath of allegiance, and made affidavit in open court of the possession of the property mentioned. They may hold civil and military offices, or places of trust under the King, his heirs and successors; and may take degrees and professorships, or be fellows of any College to be hereafter founded, provided such College be a Member of the University of Dublin, and not founded exclusively for the education of Roman Catholics, &c. &c. They are not to sit in Parliament, nor to hold any office therein, nor any of the great offices in the State, such as Lord Lieutenant, Lord Chancellor, Judge, &c. &c. nor Postmaster General, Master and Lieutenant of the Ordnance, Commander in Chief of the Forces, Generals on the Staff, and Sheriffs and Sub-Sheriffs, &c. &c. Popish Priests must not celebrate marriage between Protestant and Protestant, nor between a Protestant and a Papist, under forfeiture of 500*l.* From 1st June 1793, Oaths of allegiance and abjuration only necessary in taking degrees in Trinity College.[217]

Bills of a very different complexion must now be mentioned, as the production of the same session.

Among the first of these is the act 'to prevent the election or appointment of unlawful assemblies, under pretence of preparing or presenting public petitions, or other addresses to his Majesty or the parliament.' 'It enacts that all assemblies, committees, or other bodies of persons elected, or in any other manner constituted or appointed to represent, or assuming or exercising a right or authority to represent the people of this realm, or any number or description of the people of the same, or the people of any province, county, city, town, or other district within the same, under pretence of petitioning for or in any other manner procuring an alteration of matters established by law in Church or State, (save and except the knights, citizens, and burgesses elected to serve in the parliament thereof, and except the houses of convocation duly summoned by the King's writ) ARE UNLAWFUL ASSEMBLIES,' and that it is 'lawful for any Mayor, Sheriff, Justice of the Peace, or other Peace officer, and they are hereby respectively authorized within his and their respective jurisdictions to disperse all such unlawful assemblies, and if resisted to enter into the same, and to apprehend all persons offending in that behalf.' Persons giving or publishing notice of the election of such representatives, or attending, voting, or acting therein, by any means, are declared on conviction guilty of a high misdemeanor. It provides that it shall not affect elections made of bodies corporate; nor be construed 'in any manner to prevent or impede the undoubted right of his Majesty's subjects of this realm to petition his Majesty, or both houses, or either house of parliament for redress of any public grievance.'

The objections to this law are so many and so obvious, it is conceived in a spirit so contrary to the practice of both kingdoms and the present one in Great Britain, and so impolitic in itself, that no doubt can be entertained but the sense of the nation will from session to session urge and effect its repeal.

Has it not been observed that delegated or select bodies, taken out of greater ones, are always more moderate and sometimes more wise than their principals? When an immense concourse assembled, might be ready to run into excesses leading to Revolution itself, a delegated assembly would temper popular fury, for it would consist of persons interested in the public peace, as men of character, fortune, and education. The only other remarks that shall here be made on this law are – That it was not dictated by the genius of the constitution, because every avenue to the throne should be free as the air we breathe; a right guaranteed to us time immemorial –

Those grievances which are suffered to vent themselves in unrestrained complaints, and in such forms as the subject prefers, seldom produce insurrection or disorder; while those which are for a time pent up within the public breast, burst out in acts of rash but irresistible violence.[218]

The Gun-powder bill partakes of the spirit of the former, but as it is in force only till the 1st of January 1794, it is presumed it will not be revived. It ordains, under severe penalties on the importer and master of the vessel, that no person shall import ordnance, guns, pistols, gun-locks, swords, bayonets, pikes, spears, balls, gunpowder, or military accoutrements, without a licence from the Chief Governor of the kingdom or his Secretary, or the commissioners of the revenue, or any two of them, or the Master General, or Lieutenant General, or Board of his Majesty's Ordnance. Neither cannon, arms, gun-locks, balls, or gun-powder can be removed from one part of the kingdom to another, without similar licence, or one from any two of the commissioners of the revenue: any officer of the revenue, any Justice of the peace, or peace officer, may search for and seize all such cannon, arms, gun-powder, &c. removed without such license, provided always that these restrictions shall not extend to prevent any person from carrying arms for the defence of his person, or for sporting, as by law he might before this act. No person is allowed to keep more than four pounds of powder, nor to keep in his possession any cannon or other ordnance, without licence of the Lord Lieutenant, or his secretary, or any two of the Commissioners of the revenue, and any justice of peace may seize or by his warrant cause such to be seized, as are kept without said licence.

No person can keep for, or expose to sale any cannon or other ordnance, guns, bayonets, or gun-powder, &c. without a licence from any two of the Commissioners of the revenue, or the Collector of the district. Justices are impowered to enter and search, (or to

grant warrants so to do) any house, shop, place, &c. where he sus-
pects that such arms, gun powder, &c. may be deposited without
license.[219]

*   *   *

Whoever takes a general retrospect of the historical deduction,
contained in this and the preceding number, perceives that the
spirit of both the commons and the people, has greatly encreased.
Without suffering himself to be depressed by temporary infringements of his rights, he may find solid ground for PERSEVERANCE,
as CONSTANCY in the pursuit of rational measures, must ultimately
be omnipotent – A mass of evidence proves that the prosperity,
power, and influence of Ireland, are in a state of progressive
improvement. That they have not during the last eleven years,
advanced with tardy step, will be apparent, when we recollect how
short a period has elapsed since we had any constitution to treat of;
since even the Protestant body could be roused from a state of
torpor, to consider the national claims of the nation. Let us reli-
giously keep within the pale of the constitution, and carry along
with us the honesty, spirit, and intelligence of the country, both in
and out of parliament. All these we had, in the memorable year
EIGHTY-TWO. Then, the virtue of the kingdom in whatever rank it
could be found, was wisely collected in a point, and rose superior to
controul. These we were in possession of till lately, and if we have
lost them for a season, it behoves us to seek for their restoration, as
well as in future carefully to avoid whatever led to the effect.

It was remarked by Mr FLOOD, with his usual acumen, that it is
our national character to be prompt in entering on great enterprizes;
but easily diverted from our object, and destitute of that steady
patience in the chace, without which it is difficult to acquire any
thing. He observed that in these respects we were outdone by our

English neighbours, who seldom relinquish measures which they have once taken up with spirit. His observation deserves the attention of Irishmen.[220]

We shall take leave of our subject, in the classical language of JUNIUS; to whose exalted mind, a veneration of the constitution appeared to be perfectly consistent with the purest principles of freedom.

No man [says that elegant and nervous writer] laments more sincerely than I do, the unhappy differences which have arisen among the friends of the people, and divided them from each other. The cause undoubtedly suffers, as well by the diminution of that strength, which union carries with it, as by the separate loss of personal reputation, which every man sustains, when his character and his conduct are frequently held forth in odious or contemptible colours. These differences are only advantageous to the common enemy of the country. – It is time for those who really mean the *cause* and the *people*, who have no view to private advantage, and who have virtue enough to prefer the general good of the community – it is time for such men to interfere. – What remains to be done concerns the collective body of the people. They are now to determine for themselves, whether they will firmly and constitutionally assert their rights or make an humble slavish surrender of them. We owe it to our ancestors to preserve entire those rights, which they have delivered to our care; we owe it to our posterity, not to suffer our dearest inheritance to be destroyed.[221]

Notes

NOTES TO INTRODUCTION

Abbreviations:
NLI   National Library of Ireland
PRONI   Public Record Office of Northern Ireland

1   The debates on the Catholic question took place on 28 January 1792. For a discussion of them, see I. R. McBride, *Scripture Politics, Ulster Presbyterianism and Irish Radicalism in the Late Eighteenth Century* (Oxford, 1998), pp. 170–5. For Bruce's 'Strictures on the Test, taken by certain of the societies if the United Irishmen' and Drennan's replies, see *Belfast News-Letter*, 10 Feb.–27 Mar. 1792.

2   A. T. Q. Stewart, 'The transformation of Presbyterian radicalism in the North of Ireland, 1798–1825' (MA thesis, Queen's University, Belfast, 1956); R. F. Holmes, 'From Rebels to Unionists: The political transformation of Ulster's Presbyterians', in R. Hanna (ed.), *The Union: Essays on Ireland and the British Connection* (Newtownards, 2001), pp. 34–47. For the involvement of former Volunteers in the yeomanry, see A. Blackstock, *'Double Traitors': The Belfast Volunteers and Yeoman, 1778–1828* (Belfast, 2002).

3   *DNB*. Also, A. Gordon, 'William Bruce DD', in *Belfast Literary Society: An Historical Sketch* (Belfast, 1902), p. 31. For the Bruce family, see Classon Porter, *The Seven Bruces: Presbyterian Ministers in Ireland in Six Successive Generations* (Belfast, 1885).

4   For the importance of Drennan and his relationship with Bruce see, A. T. Q. Stewart, *A Deeper Silence: The Hidden Origins of the United Irishmen* (Belfast, 1993).

5   C. Robbins, *The Eighteenth-Century Commonwealthman: Studies in the Transmission, Development, and Circumstances of English Liberal Thought from the Restoration of Charles II Until the War with the Thirteen Colonies* (Cambridge, Mass., 1959), pp. 168–171; M. Brown, *Francis Hutcheson in Dublin, 1719–30: The Crucible of His Thought* (Dublin, 2002); Stewart, *A Deeper Silence*, pp. 72, 87–9, 92–4, 112; I. R. McBride, 'The school of virtue, Francis Hutcheson, Irish Presbyterians and the Scottish Enlightenment', in D. G. Boyce, R. Eccleshall and V. Geoghegan (eds), *Political Thought in Ireland since the Seventeenth Century* (London, 1993), pp. 73–99. The 'new light' dissenters, exponents of the movement of 'rational dissent', defended the right of private judgement in opposition to Church

authority and did not subscribe to the Westminster Confession of faith, hence the label 'non-subscribing'.

6   Alexander Stewart, the grandfather of Lord Castlereagh, was also closely attached to this set and was particularly close to William Bruce the publisher and Hutcheson, over whose grave he had a monument built (Robbins, *Eighteenth-Century Commonwealthman*), p. 171.

7   William Drennan, quoted in Robbins, *Eighteenth-Century Commonwealthman*, pp. 168–9.

8   Charlemont had expressed alarm at Bruce's early radicalism in the 1780s and, despite his friendship with Haliday, scolded the latter for his lack of moderation in framing the resolutions of the Northern Whig Club in 1790. For Charlemont see, M. McCarthy (ed.), *Lord Charlemont and His Circle* (Dublin, 2001).

9   For the Joys, see M. McNeill, *The life and times of Mary Ann McCracken* (Dublin, 1960). For Henry Joy jun., see I. Ward, 'Henry Joy', *Belfast Literary Society: An Historical Sketch* (Belfast, 1902) p. 41.

10   J. Gray, 'A tale of the two newspapers: the contest between the *Belfast News-Letter* and the *Northern Star* in the 1790s', in J. Gray and W. McCann (eds), *An Uncommon Bookman: Essays in Memory of J. R. R. Adams* (Belfast, 1996), pp. 175–98.

11   *Historical Collections Relative to the Town of Belfast from the Earliest Period to the Union with Great Britain* (Belfast, 1817).

12   *Joy MSS* 10, 11, Linen Hall Library, Belfast. For the 'new' British History as applied to the case of Ulster, see Patrick Griffin, 'Defining the limits of Britishness: the "new" British history and the meaning of the revolution settlement in Ireland for Ulster's Presbyterians', *Journal of British Studies* 39, 3 (July, 2000), pp. 263–87.

13   See for example, H. Cunningham, 'The language of patriotism, 1750–1914', *History Workshop*, no. 12, pp. 8–33; P. Spence, *The Birth of Romantic Radicalism: War, Popular Politics and English Radical Reformism* (Hampshire, 1996). Similarities between Belfast moderate politics and the constitution-inspired, reformist loyalism of Cartwright is particularly striking. Bruce's 1803 sermon, *The Christian Soldier* (Belfast) can be compared to Cartwright's 1803–4 writings, calling forth 'the Military Energies of the Constitution' to resist French invasion.

14   Joy to Haliday, 3 Feb. 1800, *Joy MSS* 9. Joy seems to have good reason to believe this story. Adams (1735–1826) was an expert on European affairs and his posting at the Hague in 1780–2 would have coincided with Maclaine's. In 1746 Maclaine had become assistant to his maternal uncle, Robert Milling, a pastor of the Scottish church at the Hague, before taking over that role himself. He was one time preceptor to the Prince of Orange. 'I was as great a Whig', he wrote to Joy, 'as Pym, Hampden or my Idol King William, until Lady *Whiggism* was bit by the mad dogs of the French Revolution and debauched by the [Lord] Fitzgeralds [and Arthur] O'Connors, but since that time I have been if not verging towards *Toryism*, yet lending a docile ear to the sedate and prudent friends of Monarchy'. Maclaine to Joy [no date, probably 1803], *Joy MSS*, 9

15   Many United Irishmen, particularly those based in Philadelphia, established themselves in the radical wing of the Republican party and contributed to Thomas Jefferson's 'second American Revolution of 1800', brought about by the defeat of Adams. See D. A. Wilson, *United Irishmen, United States: Immigrant Radicals in the Early Republic* (Ithaca and London, 1998); M. J. Bric, 'Ireland, America and the transformation of US politics, 1738–1800', in T. Bartlett, D. Dickson, D. Keogh and K. Whelan (eds), *1798: A Bicentenary Perspective* (Dublin, 2003), pp. 620–33.

16 'It was natural that an enthusiastic love of Gallic emancipation should widely extend itself, and in no tract of country more than in the *North of Ireland*, that Nidus of American Independence'. See essay No. XIII of 'Thoughts on the British Constitution'.

17 For example, S. Small, 'The twisted roots of Irish patriotism: Anglo-Irish political thought in the late eighteenth century', *Eire-Ireland* 35 (Fall/Winter, 2000–1); N. J. Curtin, *The United Irishmen: Popular Politics in Ulster and Dublin, 1791–1798* (Oxford, 1998); McBride, *Scripture Politics*; K. Whelan, *The Tree of Liberty: Radicalism, Catholicism and the construction of Irish Liberty, 1760–1830* (Cork, 1996).

18 R. R. Madden, *The United Irishmen: Their Lives and Times* (Dublin, n.d.), pp. 132–3.

19 McBride, *Scripture Politics*, pp. 176–7. There is also one reference in Stewart, *A Deeper Silence*, p. 125.

20 S. J. Connolly (ed.), *Political Ideas in Eighteenth-Century Ireland* (Dublin, 2000); D. G. Boyce, R. Eccleshall and V. Geoghegan (eds), *Political Discourse in Seventeenth- and Eighteenth-Century Ireland* (Dublin, 2000).

21 See T. Dunn, *Rebellions: Memoir, Memory and 1798* (Dublin, 2004) and R. F. Foster, 'Remembering 1798', in I. McBride (ed.), *History and Memory in Modern Ireland* (Cambridge, 2001), pp. 67–94. For a recent reply to Foster see Bartlett, 'Telling tales and making it up in Ireland', *Times Literary Supplement* (25 Jan. 2002).

22 J. Smyth, *The Men of No Property, Irish Radicals and Popular Politicisation in the Late Eighteenth Century* (Hampshire, 1999), p.79.

23 A recent exception is U. Gillen, 'Ulster liberal opinion and France, *c.*1787–96', *Irish History: a Research Yearbook*, no. 2 (2003), pp. 22–31. For the Parliamentary fortunes of Irish Whigs, see also N. Curtin, '"A perfect liberty": the rise and fall of the Irish Whigs, 1789–97', in Boyce et al., *Political Discourse*, pp. 270–89.

24 J. Quinn, 'Theobald Wolfe Tone and the historians', *Irish Historical Studies*, no. 124 (May, 2000), pp. 113–28.

25 For the authoritative account of the genesis of this debate, see T. Bartlett, *The Fall and Rise of the Irish Nation: the Catholic question, 1690–1830* (Dublin, 1992).

26 *Belfast News-Letter*, 17 July 1792.

27 T. Bartlett (ed.), *Life of Theobald Wolfe Tone, compiled and arranged by William Theobald Tone* (Dublin, 1998), pp. 126, 144, xix. It should also be noted that even such an iconic 'enlightenment' figure as Voltaire was denounced by later Irish Catholic–nationalist commentators for his description of the 1641 Irish massacre of Protestants, in which he was charged with using the most exaggerated figures for casualties, while passing over grievances such as the penal laws. The same charge was also made against David Hume. See R. E. Ward, 'A letter from Ireland: a little known attack on David Hume's *History of England*', in *Eighteenth-Century Ireland* 2 (1987), pp. 196–7.

28 The Catholic Relief Act granted Catholics the right to vote (but not to sit in Parliament) and access to all but the highest legal positions in the state. For Joy's support for Grattan's Bill for further relief, see *Belfast News-Letter*, 8 May 1795. 'There was surely no reason to despair of ultimate success . . . never had any measure more of reason and ability to second it than is now ranged on the Catholic side'. For a further exposition of his position, see the author's preface.

29 The case of the 1798 rising in Wexford and the relative importance of sectarianism there is a particularly potent area of debate. See D. Keogh and N. Furlong (eds), *The Mighty Wave: The 1798*

Rebellion in Wexford (Blackrock, 1996) and Whelan, *The Tree of Liberty*. J. S. Donnelly, 'Sectarianism in 1798 and in Catholic nationalist memory', in L. M. Geary (ed.), *Rebellion and Remembrance in Modern Ireland* (Dublin, 2001), has recently attempted to restore the sectarian dynamic in 'all its harshness, crudeness and repulsiveness', pp. 15–37.

30 'Men of middling rank among us, and the Presbyterian Ministers particularly, have used all their influence to suppress the spirit of riot . . . Individuals of every persuasion, may be found acting wrong but you may be assured that the Presbyterians, in general, will ever pursue the publick interest and welfare of their country'. Dr [William] Campbell, Armagh, to Rev. Benjamin McDowell, Mary's Abbey, Dublin, 10 Aug. 1788. *Bruce Papers*, MS 20,874(3), NLI.

31 Drennan believed 'the different parties really agree at bottom on this issue', Drennan to Sam McTier [no date] Feb. 1792, in J. Agnew (ed.), *The Drennan–McTier Letters, vol. 1, 1776–1793* (Dublin, 1998), p. 930.

32 Haliday to Charlemont, 5 Nov. 1791, *The Manuscripts and Correspondence of James, First Earl of Charlemont, vol. 2, 1784–1799*, [Historical Manuscripts Commission, Thirteenth Report] (London, 1984), p. 160.

33 Bartlett (ed.) *Life of Tone*, p. 451; Bartlett, 'Theobald Wolfe Tone: an eighteenth-century republican and separatist', *The Republic*, no. 2, (Spring/Summer 2001), pp. 38–46. For an alternative account of this period, see M. Elliott, *Wolfe Tone: Prophet of Irish Independence* (New Haven and London, 1989), pp. 172–7.

34 Stewart, *Deeper Silence*, pp. 136–9.

35 *Joy MSS* 8. See also, I. McBride, 'The harp without the crown: nationalism and republicanism in the 1790s', in Connolly (ed.), *Political Ideas in Eighteenth-Century Ireland* (Dublin, 2000), pp. 159–85. This article emphasises the importance of the popular democratic propaganda of the United Irishmen in alienating potential moderate support.

36 See for example, N. J. Curtin, 'Rebels and radicals: the United Irishmen in County Down', in L. Proudfoot (ed.), *Down: History and Society* (Dublin, 1997), pp. 267–96. Down, for example, boasted the largest number of United Irishmen of any county, estimated at over 28,000 of a population of 200,000 in the early 1790s.

37 *Belfast News-Letter*, 19 Feb. 1793.

38 *Northern Star*, 20 Feb. 1793; quoted in R. B. McDowell, *Ireland in the Age of Imperialism and Revolution, 1760–1801* (Oxford, 1979), p. 428.

39 Joseph Pollock, *Letters to the Inhabitants of the Town and Lordship of Newry* (Dublin, 1793), pp. 18, 37–42. Pollock complained of an 'unexpected' attack on his resolutions as 'too milky' by Joy. 'Mr Joy, for some time past, and till very lately indeed, had been what is called, discredited, a *moderate* . . . When accused by *him* of a want of political spirit, what must the high-flying conceive of me?'

40 Joy to Charlemont, 22 Feb. 1793, *The Manuscripts and Correspondence of James, First Earl of Charlemont, vol. 2, 1784–1799*. For the resolutions, see *Belfast News-Letter*, 19 Feb. 1793.

41 Drennan to Sam McTier, 25 Feb. 1794, *Drennan–McTier Letters, vol. 2*, p. 23.

42 Martha McTier to Drennan, 8 Feb. 1794, *Drennan–McTier Letters, vol. 1*, p. 488.

43 Charlemont, Dublin, to Joy, 18 Apr. 1794, *Joy MSS* 11.

44 McBride, *Scripture Politics*, p. 177.

45 Joy to Charlemont, 29 Apr. 1793; Charlemont to Joy, 3 May 1793, *Joy MSS* 11.

46   Joy to Charlemont, 12 Apr. 1794, *The Manuscripts and Correspondence of James, First Earl of Charlemont*, vol. 2, *1784–1799*, p. 235.

47   Bartlett (ed.), *Life of Tone*, p. 119.

48   Martha McTier to Drennan, 24 Oct. 1794, *Drennan-McTier Letters, vol. 2.*, p. 106.

49   P. Brooke, *Ulster Presbyterianism: The Historical Perspective* (Dublin, 1987), p. 126

50   *Belfast News-Letter*, 19 Nov. 1790.

51   Edmund Burke, 'Letter to Sir Hercules Langrishe' (1792), in R. B. McDowell (ed.), *The Writings and Speeches of Edmund Burke, Vol. ix, 1: The Revolutionary War, 1794–1797, 11: Ireland* (Oxford, 1991), pp. 594–639. For the dispute see M. Durey, 'The Dublin Society of United Irishmen and the politics of the Carey–Drennan dispute, 1792–1794', *Historical Journal* 37, 1 (Mar. 1994), pp. 89–111.

52   *Joy MSS* 8.

53   See Curtin, *United Irishmen*, pp. 6–21; Small, 'The twisted roots of Irish patriotism'; Bartlett, 'Theobald Wolfe Tone: an eighteenth-century republican and separatist'. For the classic account of the 'transmission' of commonwealthman ideas from the late seventeenth century to the eighteenth, see Robbins, *The Eighteenth-Century Commonwealthman*, pp. 134–76.

54   Small, 'The twisted roots of Irish patriotism'; Curtin, *United Irishmen*, p. 7.

55   See B. Worden, *Roundhead Reputations: The English Civil War and the Passions of Posterity* (London, 2001), pp. 147–81. The 'real Whig' critique was directed away from an attack on monarchy to a form of anti-clericalism, opening up the possibility of a 'patriot King'. The Belfast-based Northern Whig club was typical of many similar organisations in Britain in failing to draw a distinction between the moderate constitutionalist cause 'for which Hampden bled in the field' and the radical republican agenda for which 'Sidney died on the scaffold'. See Essay No. I also.

56   See R. Williams, *Keywords: A Vocabulary of Culture and Society* (London, 1981, 2nd edn), pp. 279–84.

57   See J. A. Epstein, 'The constitutionalist idiom: radical reasoning, rhetoric and action in early nineteenth-century England', *Journal of Social History* 23, 3 (Spring 1990), pp. 553–74.

58   J. Livesey, 'From the ancient constitution to democracy: Transformations in republicanism in the eighteenth century', in T. Bartlett, D. Dickson, D. Keogh and K. Whelan (eds), *1798: A Bicentenary Perspective* (Dublin, 2003), pp. 14–27. Eighteenth-century republicanism was 'a theory to define the best kind of political culture for a modern commercial nation', never simply 'a variant of nationalism'.

59   See W. Doyle, 'Father of the Republic', *Times Literary Supplement* (12 Sept. 2001); P. Brooke, *Ulster Presbyterianism: The Historical Perspective* (Dublin, 1987), p. 177; Curtin, *United Irishmen*, p. 13.

60   J. Scott, *England's Troubles: Seventeenth Century English Political Instability in a European Context* (Cambridge, 2000), pp. 290–341; J. G. A. Pocock and G. J. Schochet, 'Interregnum and Restoration', in Pocock and Schochet (eds), *The Varieties of British Political Thought, 1500–1800* (Cambridge, 1993), pp. 146–79. The prominent exception to this argument was James Harrington, whose projected commonwealth of Oceana contained an elaborate and precise governmental system.

61   This rested on the dominant post-classical view (derived largely from Plato and Thucydides) which regarded Athenian democracy as sheer tyrannical demagogy and saw the Spartan mixed constitution (which included a monarchy) as superior.

62   Polybius was, to some extent, rediscovered by Machiavelli and became crucial to many seventeenth-century classical republican thinkers (J. Scott, *England's Troubles: Seventeenth-Century English Political Instability in European Context* (Cambridge, 2000), pp. 37, 293, 302, 328) and was also used in James Harrington's 1656 radical republican text *The Commonwealth of Oceana*, which Bruce's uncle had republished in 1737. For the continued importance of these thinkers and their use of Polybius in the eighteenth century, see J. G. A. Pocock, 'Machiavelli, Harrington and English political ideologies in the eighteenth century', *William and Mary Quarterly* 3rd ser., 22, 4 (Oct. 1965), pp. 549–83.

63   Drennan, quoted in S. J. Connolly, 'Precedent and principle: the patriots and their critics', in Connolly (ed.), *Political Ideas in Eighteenth-Century Ireland* (Dublin, 2000), pp. 130–58.

64   John Adams, *An Answer to Pain's [sic] Rights of Man* (Dublin, 1973). Adams is referred to directly in Essay No. VII.

65   See, Worden, *Roundhead Reputations*, pp. 210–11. It should be noted Adams stood for a more conservative federalist view of the American polity which held that the propertied should have greater influence (maintained by checks and balances such as the indirectly elected Senate and the Electoral College in the Presidency), as distinct from the more democratic Jeffersonian agenda.

66   John Lawless, *The Belfast Politics Enlarged; Being a Compendium of the Political History of Ireland, For the Last Forty Years* (Belfast, 1818), p. 9. See also Lawless's political magazine, *The Ulster Register*, 21 Mar. 1818. For numerous references to Lawless's career, see D. Keenan, *The Grail of Catholic Emancipation, 1793–1829* (Philadelphia, 2002).

67   Henry Joy and William Bruce, *Belfast Politics*, 'United Irish Reprints', No. 4 (Belfast, 1974), p. 6.

68   See J. Kelly, 'Public and political opinion in Ireland and the idea of an Anglo-Irish Union', in Boyce et al., *Political Discourse*, pp. 110–41.

69   Owen Roe O'Neill [Joseph Pollock], *Letters to the Men of Ireland* (Dublin, 1779).

70   Joseph Pollock, *Letters to the Inhabitants of Newry* (Dublin, 1793), p. 152. Pollock is usually seen as one of the most prominent old Volunteers to adopt a 'conservative' path in the 1790s but he defended his consistency at the Dungannon Volunteer Convention of 1793 with a critique of the French Revolution for becoming embroiled in international disputes, despite the pacifist rhetoric of 1789: 'War was to cease, the wolf to dwell with the lamb and the infant to lead the young lion!'

71   Castlereagh to 'My Dearest Doctor' Haliday, 27 Feb. 1792, *Castlereagh Papers*, D/3030/37, PRONI. For Irish experience in a European context, see also Brendan Simms, 'Continental analogies with 1798: Revolution or counter-revolution', in Thomas Bartlett, David Dickson, Daire Keogh and Kevin Whelan (eds), *1798: A Bicentenary Perspective* (Dublin, 2003), pp. 577–95.

72   Castlereagh to 'My Dearest Doctor' Haliday, 27 Feb. 1792, *Castlereagh Papers*, D/3030/37.

73   Haliday to Charlemont, [no date] Aug. 1792, *The Manuscripts and Correspondence of James, First Earl of Charlemont, vol. 2, 1784–1799*, p. 247. Castlereagh was obviously still concerned about the opinions of his former reforming friends. 'Pray', he asked his wife, 'what does Haliday say in cold blood?' [ante 23 Sept.] 1796 *Castlereagh Papers*, D3030/T/(MC3/290) PRONI. Indeed, just a month before the first French invasion scare, when a French fleet arrived at Bantry Bay off the west coast of Ireland, he was even able to have 'a good deal of funny conversation' with a group of radicals whom he passed a few miles from Belfast. Castlereagh to his wife, 7[or 8] Nov. 1796, *Castlereagh Papers*, D/3030/T/(MC3/290) PRONI.

74   See for example, John Yates of Liverpool, to Bruce, 4 April 1799, *Bruce Papers*, T/3041/1/E125, PRONI. 'The result of reasoning of the most candid minds with which I am acquainted here is that more complete union or entire separation is necessary and as the latter seems, under present circumstances, neither practicable nor desirable, the former appears to be highly expedient'. For the close ties between the United Irishmen and the French, see M. Elliot, *Partners in Revolution, The United Irishmen and France* (New Haven and London, 1982).

75   Pollock's *Letters to the Inhabitants of the Town and Lordship of Newry* (Dublin, 1793), p. 102. He questioned 'how far' the United Irishmen, for all their talk of reform of the constitution and the existing body politic, were 'attached to the patient'. For the various versions of the constitution and the variety of those groups that called on it, see S. Small, *Political Thought in Ireland, 1776–1798: Republicanism, Patriotism and Radicalism* (Oxford, 2002).

76   C. Kidd, *Subverting Scotland's Past; Scottish whig historians and the creation of an Anglo–British identity, 1689–1830* (Cambridge, 1993), p. 211.

77   See D. Armitage, 'A patriot for whom? The afterlives of Bolingbroke's patriot king', *Journal of British Studies* 36, 4 (Oct. 1997), pp. 397–418.

78   Kidd, *Subverting Scotland's Past*, pp. 205–15. For an introduction to the importance of these themes in Irish history, see I. McBride, '"The common name of Irishman": Protestantism and patriotism in eighteenth century Ireland', in T. Claydon and I. McBride (eds), *Protestantism and National Identity in Britain and Ireland, c.1650–1850* (Cambridge, 1998), pp. 236–61.

79   *Belfast News-Letter*, 17 July 1792. See also R. Romani, *National Character and Public Spirit in Britain and France, 1750–1914* (Cambridge, 2002), pp. 19–62.

80   See J. Rendall, *The Origins of the Scottish Enlightenment* (London, 1978), pp. 124–37. In Adam Ferguson's words, 'men stumble upon institutions'.

81   William Campbell, *A Vindication of the Principles and Character of the Presbyterians of Ireland* (Dublin, 1787). This characterised the Presbyterian as the 'father' to the Constitution, the Protestant as the 'child' and the Catholic as 'not an Enemy'. See also Patrick Griffin, 'Defining the limits of Britishness: The "new" British history and the meaning of the Revolution Settlement in Ireland for Ulster's Presbyterians', *Journal of British Studies* 39, 3 (July 2000), 263–87.

82   C. Kidd, 'North Britishness and the nature of eighteenth-century British patriotism', *The Historical Journal* 39, 2 (1996), pp. 361–82. This argues that an 'Anglo-British' form of patriotism was a common feature of the British Atlantic world and manifested itself in America, Scotland and Ireland in a longing for the full enjoyment of English liberties.

NOTES TO BELFAST POLITICS

1   The compiler was most likely Joy.

2   Although the 'proceedings' alluded to here are not included in this edition, this is an important passage. By the 'majority', the writer meant the radicals of the town, who had defeated the moderates (the 'minority') in a public debate in Belfast on 28 January 1792 on a resolution in favour of Catholic emancipation. The radicals successfully inserted the *caveat* that the removal of penal laws should be 'immediate' ahead of the moderate suggestion that it should take place 'from time to time, and as speedily as the circumstances of the whole country, and the welfare of the whole kingdom will permit'. For a discussion of this debate, see McBride, *Scripture Politics*, pp. 171–3.

3 The writer of the first number was probably Bruce. The 'friend' was probably Joy, or perhaps Dr Haliday.

4 This was a reference to a public correspondence between a 'PORTIA' and 'Mr Jones' which appeared on Parliamentary reform and the Catholic question in the *Belfast News-Letter* in the early 1790s.

5 The Dublin Corporation and the Grand Juries, conservative and largely anti-Catholic, were for a long time regarded as the bastion of Episcopalian Church interests and Irish Toryism. See J. Hill, *From Patriots to Unionists: Dublin Civic Politics and Irish Patriotism, 1660–1840* (Oxford, 1997).

6 The Catholic Relief Act (9 Apr. 1793, 33 Geo. III, c.2) is what had been 'accomplished'. It granted Catholics the right to vote (but not to sit in Parliament) and access to all but the highest legal positions in the state. Joy publicly welcomed the Act and called for further measures in his penultimate *Belfast News-Letter* editorial on 8 May 1795.

7 One of the central tenets of the United Irish political strategy was to unite Protestant reformers and Catholics emancipationists in one great movement for reform. As Joy and Bruce were aware, this tactic had been mooted by the Volunteers for over a decade and had contributed to the divisions that had caused the Volunteer movement to 'run out of steam' in the mid-1780s (McBride, *Scripture Politics*, pp. 152–61). Even among United Irishmen in the 1790s, tensions continued between those who saw Catholic relief as a priority and those who regarded Parliamentary reform as the most important aim. See for example, M. Durey, 'The Dublin Society of United Irishmen and the politics of the Carey–Drennan dispute, 1792–1794', *Historical Journal* 37, 1 (Mar. 1994), pp. 89–111.

8 This included suppression of the Volunteers' right to assemble, a Gunpowder bill to regulate holding of arms by private citizens, drafting of the militia into Ulster and the introduction of martial law in Belfast, assisted by a growing network of spies and informers. While 'the constitution I almost idolise', Joy complained to Charlemont, its abuse 'startles some of the oldest, warmest and best friends of the Principles of the Government we live under' (Joy to Charlemont, 29 Apr. 1793, *Joy MSS* 11).

9 For an account of the last Volunteer Convention, at Dungannon in February 1793, see Stewart, *A Deeper Silence*, p. 327, or McBride, *Scripture Politics*, pp. 174–5.

10 For the moderates, United Irish Societies and secret cabals were a significant departure from the old Volunteer civic humanist tradition of a distinctly public and participatory form of patriotism.

11 Note that in 1794, Joy and Bruce seemed to regard the Union as the option of those afraid of the consequences of the continued polarisation of Irish politics, but at this stage they distance themselves from that position. They also refused to abandon their demands for Parliamentary reform at any stage in the 1790s, even when enrolling in the militia. 'We', insisted a group calling themselves the 'Friends of Parliamentary Reform' which included Joy and Bruce, 'who have always sought for reform, within the limits of the constitution . . . have determined not to slacken our Exertions' (*Belfast News-Letter*, 25 Jan. 1793). Haliday also later confirmed to Charlemont that the Belfast merchant yeomanry corps were still demanding reform as late as 1797. As far as he was aware, 'none of the *soi-disant* yeoman have breathed a syllable respecting our wrongs, except the yeoman of Belfast', 13 July 1797, in *The Manuscripts and Correspondence of James, First Earl of Charlemont, vol. 2, 1784–1799*, p. 303.

12 This is probably a reference to Prime Minister William Pitt's involvement in putting pressure on the Irish government to push through the Catholic Relief Act of 1793. 'The British

Government, which for a year had been pressing the Irish Administration to conciliate the Catholics by generous concessions, now exercised all the leverage at its command, and at the beginning of 1793 the Irish Administration introduced a wider relief bill which granted the Irish Catholics the franchise and admission to office under the Crown, with the exception of a number of senior posts'. This is the account given in R. B. McDowell (ed.), *The Writings and Speeches of Edmund Burke, Vol. IX, I: The Revolutionary War, 1794–1797, II: Ireland* (Oxford, 1991), p. 419.

13 The Belfast and Dublin branches of the United Irishmen.

14 This was a typical critique of the use of a government-controlled, centralised police force. Both moderates and radicals associated it with systems of Continental despotism and regarded as a threat to civil liberty.

15 One of Joy's central arguments against an immediate and full measure of emancipation was what he saw as a lack of 'enlightenment' beyond Belfast and Dublin. For all the excitement in these metropolitan centres, the 1790s also witnessed a worrying increase of sectarian violence in many parts of the country, against which the Volunteers liked to style themselves as the moderate bulwark. In July 1792 he had spoken about the need for their resolutions to be 'moderate and precise; such as to foster the growing sense of liberality among our Protestant brethren, who are yet unprepared to go hand in hand with the inhabitants of this land in an instantaneous and unlimited change' (*Belfast News-Letter*, 17 July 1792). For the intensification of religious tension in some areas, see T. Bartlett, 'Religious rivalries in France and Ireland in the age of the French Revolution', *Eighteenth-Century Ireland* 6 (Dublin, 1991), pp. 57–76; P. Gibbon, 'The origins of the Orange Order and the United Irishmen', *Economy and Society* 1, 2 (1972), pp. 134–64.

16 An article on Joy's tenure as editor, after he had left the *News-Letter*, argued that 'in principle', he had been among the 'most zealous advocates' of Catholic relief 'before many of their present friends has parted with . . . [their] prejudices' (15 May 1795). Privately, however, he admitted to not being so 'sanguine' about the 1793 Act as many of his townsmen because, as Burke had calculated, it had taken the pressure off the government to grant a measure of Parliamentary reform. It had 'so completely disengaged the question of their freedom (the Catholics) from that of an improvement in the Representation. Had they gone hand in hand, our hope might have been higher', Joy to Charlemont, 29 Apr. 1793, *Joy MSS* 11.

17 The notion that Catholics were more naturally disposed to monarchical (sometimes absolutist) systems of government and had generally conservative political tendencies was a common prejudice in late eighteenth-century Ireland. Edmund Burke's 1792 *Letter to Sir Hercules Langrishe* had done nothing to allay these suspicions by arguing that in the event of a Relief Act, the new Catholic voters would act as a conservative bulwark against radical Dissenters (see Durey, 'The Dublin Society of United Irishmen and the politics of the Drennan–Carey dispute'). For many, however, Catholic involvement in the French Revolution had exploded this myth; this was certainly an argument employed by Wolfe Tone in *An Argument on Behalf of the Catholics of Ireland (1791)*, ed. B. Clifford (Belfast, 1992).

18 William Drennan's sister, Martha McTier, made similar complaints about the state of Belfast politics after the victory of the radicals over the moderates on the Catholic question. She complained of the conduct of some of the radicals 'puffed up by self confidence . . . the advantage they have gained over the more respected inhabitants by being on the popular side . . . [has] given them a boasting manner and dictatorial speech . . . avowing in a most impudent manner republican sentiments and

talking of kings as if they were to be their butchers' (Martha McTier to Drennan, 25 Dec. 1792, *The Drennan–McTier Letters*, vol. 2, p. 451). McBride suggests that the moderate–radical division also reflected social distinctions between the longer established 'mercantile elite' and a more radical class of 'upwardly mobile men', often immigrants from the countryside (*Scripture Politics*, pp. 172–3).

19   Due to the fact that Belfast was the pocket borough of Lord Donegall, the elections for the county of Down had for some time been regarded as a crucial political battlefield for local reformers. It was for a Down seat that Lord Castlereagh had been returned as a reformer in 1790. See N. Curtin, 'Rebels and radicals in County Down, 1801–1921', in L. Proudfoot (ed.), *Down: History and Society* (Dublin, 1997), pp. 267–98.

20   Dublin Castle, seat of the Irish administration.

21   This refers to the significant body of reformers who had followed the moderate line on the Catholic question and subsequently formed themselves into groups like 'the Friends of Parliamentary Reform' (*Belfast News-Letter*, 25 Jan. 1793) or the 'Association of the Friends of the Constitution, Liberty and Peace'. The latter stressed that 'the abuses of our constitution should not make us forget that we *have* one' (*Belfast News-Letter*, 8 Feb. 1793).

22   It was a civic humanist commonplace that the Caesarean precedent of using private troops (the Praetorian bands) rather than a public militia was one of the main reasons for the emergence of despotism and the fall of the Roman republic. The potential tyranny of mercenaries over unarmed citizens was a mainstay of civic humanist and classical republican discourse, an idea enshrined in the American constitutional amendment guaranteeing the right of citizens to bear arms as part of a 'well ordered militia'.

23   In the 1640s the 'Belfast presbytery' had provoked a public dispute with John Milton after they had condemned the execution of Charles I (Stewart, *A Deeper Silence*, p. 107). It was common for Presbyterians to refer back to their resistance to Cromwell in the seventeenth century (a 'true-blue Presbyterian loyalty'), particularly when responding to suspicions that they were anti-monarchic.

24   Due to the self-confessed inability of the Irish government to protect Ireland's shores, Belfast had been among the first towns to arm against the threat of French invasion earlier in the century. It was for this reason widely regarded as the home of the Volunteer movement. See Stewart in *A Deeper Silence*, pp. 1–20.

25   Niccolo Machiavelli (1469–1527) wrote *Storie Fiorentine* at the request of Pope Clement VII. It was a history of Florence from the fall of the Roman Empire until 1492.

26   This was the pen name used by Henry St John, Viscount Bolingbroke (1678–1751) in his *Remarks on the History of England by Humphrey Oldcastle* (1730). Bolingbroke, a prominent English political philosopher, is generally thought to have contributed to something of a 'conservative enlightenment' in the eighteenth century. See A. Hassel (ed.), *Bolingbroke's Political Writings: The Conservative Enlightenment* (Houndmills, 1997). On the other hand, David Armitage has argued for a reappraisal of Bolingbroke's influence on eighteenth-century patriotism. This is intended to qualify the notion that his writings were instrumental in the 'rightward drift' of patriotism towards a more conservative, or jingoistic, nationalism. See Armitage, 'A patriot for whom? The afterlives of Bolingbroke's patriot king', *Journal of British Studies* 36, 4 (Oct. 1997), pp. 397–418. The extensive use of Bolingbroke made by the Belfast moderates in this text certainly supports that argument.

27   For Charlemont and his links to the authors, see introduction. It is worth noting that the first half of the original edition (the collection of resolutions and debates which are not included here)

was dedicated to Dr Alexander Haliday, 'a lover of liberty, and of letters: uniting wit, chaste as brilliant, with the virtues of a patriot, friend and beloved physician'.

28 This essay appeared as the first of the series in the *Belfast News-Letter*, 7 Dec. 1792. In the previous issue, on 4 Dec., the paper had printed an address from the Dublin Society of the Irishmen, with William Drennan in the chair, to Scottish reformers. This called for a common resistance to the 'haughty monopoly' of England. It was against this background that the authors of this essay reiterated their preference for the 'British' form of government. The quotations from Millar and Oldcastle did not appear in the original edition.

29 John Millar, *An Historical View of the English Government from the Settlement of the Saxons in Britain to the Revolution of 1688 to which are subjoined Dissertations connected with the History of the Revolution to the Present Time* (1787). A student of Adam Smith and chair of civil law at Glasgow University, Millar (1735–1801) was a central figure in the Scottish Enlightenment. He is sometimes identified as a pioneer of sociology because of his emphasis on the importance of the past, particularly the material base of society, in understanding present social forms and systems of government. See W. Lehmann, *John Millar of Glasgow, 1735–1801: his life and thought and his contributions to sociological analysis* (London, New York and Cambridge, 1960).

30 This reference to a 'great Civilian' seems to refer to an exponent of civil law, as opposed to the common law tradition, which Bruce and Joy believed was one of the most favourable aspects of the organic growth of the British constitution. For the continued importance of the civil law tradition, particularly in the Scottish Universities, see D. L. Carey Miller and R. Zimmerman (eds), *The Civilian Tradition in Scots Law* (Berlin, 1997).

31 Joy was clearly concerned about the anti-monarchical leanings of some radicals. He retained one radical pamphlet circulated in Belfast in the mid-1790s as evidence of the type of propaganda 'circulated by the United Irishmen among the common people' to turn 'regal govt. into contempt'. 'The children's catechism' denounced the King as a 'German bastard' and declared 'God save the King! Ha! Ha! Ha!'. *Joy MSS* 8.

32 Runnymede was the place where the Magna Carta, the charter which secured the rights of English nobles, was sealed by King John in 1215.

33 The Duke of Hereford (1367–1413) led a successful revolt against King Richard II in 1399. Richard surrendered within a month and Parliament confirmed Hereford as King Henry IV the same year.

34 These were the three martyrs of the seventeenth-century Whig cause for both radical and moderate Whigs. John Hampden (1594–1643) was a great Parliamentarian opponent of Charles I and died on the battlefield during the English civil war. Lord William Russell (1693–83) was one of the strongest advocates for the removal of James from the succession to Charles II's throne. In 1683 he was implicated in the Rye House plot to assassinate James and Charles and subsequently beheaded. Algernon Sidney (1622–83), a theoretical republican, was also beheaded for alleged involvement in the Rye House plot.

35 This is probably a reference to John Louis De Lome (1741–1806), another Enlightenment philosopher and writer of *The Constitution of England or an account of the English Government* (1771). A Dublin edition of this text appeared in 1775.

36 For the importance of these figures to the cause of Parliamentary reform, see No. IX.

37 Initial delight at the first French Revolutionary constitution gave way to a great sense of frustration among moderates at the continued suspension of that constitution by successive

revolutionary factions. In particular, their attitude towards France visibly cooled in early 1793 during the King's trial. The moderate Association of the Friends of the Constitution, Liberty and Peace argued that 'we can have no national temptation to encourage or encounter the evils which have flown from a total want of constitution in a neighbouring country' (*Belfast News-Letter*, 8 Feb. 1793). Joy's private jottings for 1794 further confirmed the sense of exasperation, reflecting back on the 1790 Tennis Court Oath 'never to separate until the constitution should be established' as a 'strictly moral and obligatory' undertaking which 'implies no Exception, or reservation, except in the case of Irresistible Force . . . or Death'. *Joy MSS* 14.

38   This refers to John Locke's (1632–1704) construction of a constitution for newly established colonies in seventeenth-century Carolina. At the behest of his patron, the Earl of Shaftesbury, he drafted 'the Fundamental Constitutions of Carolina' which were adopted in 1669 by the eight proprietors. The colonists, however, objected to the complex scheme of proprietary control outlined by Locke, and by 1700 his plan had been completely abandoned as a viable working model. For an edition of this plan see John Locke, *Political Writings*, ed. D. Wootton (Harmondsworth, 1995). David Armitage has argued that this aspect of Locke's work has not been given its due weight in existing scholarship ('New light on Locke and Carolina', *Times Literary Supplement* no. 5299, 22 Oct 2004).

39   The 'two living characters' referred to here are almost certainly Edmund Burke and Thomas Paine (see introduction).

40   This essay appeared as the second of the series on 14 Dec. 1792. The same edition of the *Belfast News-Letter* also printed an Answer from the President of the French National Assembly to the reformers of Belfast and Sheffield who had offered their congratulations to the French revolutionaries. It is likely that Bruce and Joy picked up on the passage in the National Assembly's address which claimed that 'the principles upon which our own constitution has been founded have been discovered by the celebrated writers of your Nation'. The newspaper also contained early signs of the government crackdown on the reform movement, with a printed proclamation from the Lord Lieutenant against the Volunteers of Dublin.

41   This is the first sentence of Book III, chapter 5 of Montesquieu's *The Spirit of the Laws* (1748). This text is used throughout 'Thoughts on the British Constitution', although the authors did not always give the precise reference of the excerpt. It should be noted that the quotation which appears here was not used in the original *News-Letter* essay. Originally, the authors used two lengthier quotations, also from Montesquieu: 'One nation there is in the world that has for the direct end of its Constitution – Political Liberty'; 'Whoever shall read the admirable Treatise of Tacitus on the manners of the Germans, will find that the *English* have borrowed the idea of their political government – This beautiful system was invented in the woods'.

42   Sallust (*c.*86–35BC), Roman tribune and distinguished historian.

43   In the *Belfast News-Letter* of 18 Dec. 1792, this essay appeared in the same issue as an appeal from the United Irishmen for the support of the Volunteers of Ireland. It should be seen, therefore, as one of the opening salvos in the battle between moderates and radicals for the leadership of the reform movement. The Continental context to this essay is also important. The *News-Letter* reported that the French army had taken the citadel of Antwerp, and that in Paris republicans were putting pressure on the National Assembly to hasten the trial of the King.

44   From *The Spirit of the Laws*, Book II, chapter 6.

45 Edward VI (1537–53) was only nine years old when he succeeded Henry VIII and during his reign much of the governmental power was ceded to a Regency Council, dominated first by Duke of Somerset and then the Duke of Northumberland. This Council sought political support by forwarding the cause of a strict and conformist version of Protestantism. One of the most famous victims of this campaign was an Anabaptist woman, Jane Bocher, who was burned at the stake in 1550 for her 'heresy'. For a modern treatment of this affair, see D. MacCulloch, *Tudor Church Militant: Edward VI and the Protestant Reformation* (Harmondsworth, 1999), pp. 141, 173.

46 Lacedemon was sometimes used as another name for Sparta.

47 Aristides 'the Just' (530–486BC), respected Athenian statesman and lawmaker. He was banished under the Athenian system of ostracism in 483BC. One legend, the one which the authors seem to be referring to here, was that he was ostracised by a man who did not know him but was simply tired of hearing him called 'the Just'. Other stories point to the involvement of his political nemesis Themistocles in his banishment.

48 Publius Valerius, also known as Poplicola ('friend of the people') was one of the first republican statesmen and led the revolt against the Tarquins, the ruling family of Rome in the sixth century BC, before falling out of favour with the democrats.

49 Manlius defended the Capitol Hill of Rome against the Gaul invasion in the fourth century BC. But not long afterwards he was impeached and thrown off the Tarpeian Rock which overlooked the Roman forum.

50 The Decemvirs were a group of ten men appointed to a special judicial or executive role in the ancient Roman state.

51 For a recent and accessible account of the disputes and wars between the great leaders of Rome and their role in the downfall of the Roman Republic, see T. Holland, *Rubicon: The Triumph and Tragedy of the Roman Republic* (London, 2003).

52 This is an abbreviation of Sallust's most famous work, *Bellum Catiline*.

53 The original edition of *Belfast Politics* contained an account of a dinner held in Belfast on 3 May 1792 to celebrate the anniversary of the 1791 Polish revolution. The Bill of Government established a constitutional hereditary monarchy in place of an elective one, created a new government and made ministers of that government responsible to the Sejm (Parliament).

54 The context of the publication of this Number on 25 Dec. 1792 was dramatic. From Ireland, there was a report of the arrest of the prominent United Irishman Archibald Hamilton Rowan. From London, there was news of the trial of Thomas Paine and from Paris, further reports of the trial of the King. It should be noted that the quotations from Montesquieu which open the essay did not appear in the original edition. The quotation that originally appeared was from Montagu's *Reflections on the rise and fall of the ancient republicks, adapted to the present state of Great Britain* (London, 1759): 'The Government first instituted by Romulus, the founder of this extraordinary Empire, was that perfect sort, (as it had been termed by Dionysius and Polybius), which consisted of a due admixture of the regal, aristocratic and democratic powers'. Edward Wortley Montagu (1713–76) was a traveller and one time MP for Huntingdon.

55 *The Spirit of the Laws*, Book I, chapter 3.

56 William Pitt 'the Elder' (1708–78). See No. IX for his links to Irish reformers.

57 John Louis De Lome (1741–1806), Enlightenment philosopher, also referred to in Essay No. I.

58   The name given to a codified digest of Roman law compiled by the order of the Byzantine emperor Justinian (AD 483–565).

59   Richard II (1367–1400) faced great opposition from the nobles of England. This quotation is taken from the proceedings of the so-called 'Merciless Parliament' of 1388 which conducted a purge of government, using the weapons of appeal and impeachment against a set of royal ministers and favourites.

60   This is a reference to the events of the 'Glorious Revolution' of 1689 when the Convention Parliament convened, declared that James II's flight to France amounted to abdication and paved the way for the arrival of William of Orange. By the Declaration of Rights, the Convention Parliament laid down the main features of the revolutionary settlement, accepted by William and Mary.

61   This is one of the more radical passages in the text, rejecting any fundamental right of bishops to sit in Parliament. It caused concern among more conservative elements of the Volunteers such as Joseph Pollock. In his *Letters to the Inhabitants of the Town and Lordship of Newry* (Dublin, 1793, pp. 183–4) he had cautiously welcomed 'Thoughts on the British Constitution' for what seemed like a 'a real intention of bringing the people back to the constitution'. But while claiming that he was not one to 'revere' bishops, he doubted that this critique was advisable 'observing *the spirit of the times*'. Pollock feared 'that "the majesty of the people", once upon its legs and in motion' might just as easily decide to dispense with monarchy and aristocracy, if it countenanced such radical views on the 'spiritual lords'.

62   It is not clear from which writer this quotation was taken. The hope expressed that this work will 'survive the language it was written in' seems to suggest that this is a classical authority. The references to 'mixed' constitutions and its concern for 'barriers' and 'stability' may also suggest that the quotation is from Polybius, who is directly referred to in the next essay (see n. 65 below). A Greek historian and leading classical authority on mixed and balanced government, his work was certainly still very influential during this period and can be detected in classical republicanism, the Scottish Enlightenment and the 'founding principles' of the American constitution. See for example, G. Chinard, 'Polybius and the American Constitution', in F. Shuffleton (ed.), *The American Enlightenment* (New York, 1993), pp. 217–37.

63   The context of this essay was the debates which took place in Belfast in late December 1792 and early January 1793 over the Catholic question (see introduction and *Belfast News-Letter*, 28 Dec. 1792). While the author asserts that 'the basis of election must be extended to Roman Catholics' ('They are *men*, with all the energies of our nature'), he fails to mention his opinion on their full political emancipation: in other words, their right to sit in Parliament. Bruce and Joy were aware that they had taken up an unpopular stance in recent debates by agreeing to full political emancipation in principle, while arguing that it should be implemented 'gradually'.

64   Charles James Fox (1749–1806), English Parliamentary Whig leader, regarded by many Irish patriots as a sympathetic exponent of Ireland's rights. He spoke out against the proclamation which effectively suppressed the Volunteers in Ireland.

65   Polybius (*c.*203–122 BC). Greek historian and leading classical authority on mixed and balanced government.

66   Hengist and Horsa were the names of the two brothers who, it was believed, led the Jutish invasion of Britain and founded the kingdom of Kent in the fifth century. They are also said to have

assisted the Britons in defend themselves against the Picts and Scots to the north. The argument here is that the implicit wisdom of balanced government, as stated by Polybius, predates any exclusively Saxon understanding of the concept.

67 Marcus Tullius Cicero (*c.*106–43 BC), Roman orator, lawyer, politician and philosopher. Republican exponent of constitutional law, refused to join the Triumvirate. His life coincided with the decline and fall of the Roman Republic, which made his writings of great interest to later political theorists, particularly those dealing with republicanism.

68 The mood of this essay is one of urgency, befitting the radicalisation of politics in Ireland and the Continent. The *News-Letter* in this period contained a series of full-page reports from Paris as the trial of the King of France was drawing to its close (see for example, 15 Jan. 1793). As the quotation from Fox at the end of the essay demonstrates, it is a plea for government to 'listen' to popular grievances. 'Procrastination', as events from France seemed to confirm, was 'dangerous'.

69 Interestingly, the Swiftian language which Bolingbroke uses here was also echoed later in the 1790s in the work of conservative pamphleteer Alexander Knox, Lord Castlereagh's former secretary. The French Convention appeared to be to him 'a giant in theory and a pigmy in practice' compared to the British constitution which Bolingbroke had celebrated. See Knox, *Essays on the Political Circumstances of Ireland written during the Administration of Earl Camden* (London, 1799), p. 100.

70 David Hume (1711–76), arguably the most important philosopher of the Scottish Enlightenment. This is most likely taken from his *The History of England from the Invasion of Julius Caesar to the Revolution in 1688* (1754–62). As Kidd has shown (*Subverting Scotland's Past*, p. 211), Hume aimed to temper the myths of the English Whig tradition – Saxon laws, ancient constitutionalism, Gothicism – with an understanding of the role of contingency in the growth of English liberty. (See also, the opening quotation of No. XIX). As part of an attempt to create a more inclusive and broader constitutional discourse, this clearly appealed to the Bruce and Joy. They, like Hume, used Polybius as an exponent of the idea that a balance of power between republican and monarchical systems preserved liberty, rather than simply relying on the rhetoric of the ancient Saxon constitution. For Hume's importance to historical writing and understanding in the period, see V. G. Wexler, 'David Hume's discovery of a new scene of historical thought', *Eighteenth-Century Studies* 10, 2 (Winter, 1976–7), pp. 185–202. See also, N. Phillipson, *Hume* (London, 1989).

71 This essay actually appeared as No. IX in the newspaper series, on 12 Feb. 1793. As a defence of the British Constitution it takes on an extra significance because the *News-Letter* also contained reports of growing hostility between Britain and France and news of an embargo of French ships in London. The two footnotes which appear were also in the original edition but the section at the end, 'Additional Notes', was added at a later date.

72 They are probably referring to John Adams's *An Answer to Pain's Rights of Man*, an edition of which appeared in Dublin in 1793. For further information on their attitudes to Adams, see introduction.

73 Charles I's introduction of a forced loan on Parliament in 1627 led the Commons into the framing of a petition in 1628, outlawing non-parliamentary taxes and arbitrary imprisonment. Charles was forced to agree this as a condition of Parliament granting him a loan.

74 This refers to the Habeas Corpus Act of 1679 which tied up many of the loopholes surrounding the enforcement and operation of the rule of law. Hume discussed Habeas Corpus in chapter LXVII of his *History of England*.

75 The Bill of Rights of 1689 confirmed the Declaration of Rights. This had been presented to William and Mary on their arrival in England to take up the Crown, following the abdication of James II. It secured many ancient English rights and recited the abuses of the royal prerogative which had taken place in James II's reign. It is mentioned throughout *Belfast Politics* as a central element of the British constitution. For the basic provisions of it see No. XIV.

76 The Star Chamber was the ancient meeting place of the King's ministers but it came to be seen as a vehicle for extending the royal prerogative and was abolished by the Long Parliament in 1640. The Court of High Commission, which handled ecclesiastical issues, was also a focal point of grievance and was abolished with the Star Chamber.

77 Another reference to the Earl of Chatham, Pitt 'the Elder', rather than Pitt 'the Younger', the Prime Minister in the 1790s.

78 This section was added by the authors when the essays were collected in book form.

79 Essay No. VIII appeared originally as No. VII in the *Belfast News-Letter*, 25 Jan. 1793. As editor, Joy revealed that he would have liked to include the essay earlier but all the space in the newspaper had been taken up by a flurry of resolutions from Volunteers corps in support of Parliamentary reform. In this issue, he also printed a report of the meeting of the 'Friends of Parliamentary Reform' which was composed of the moderate men of the town who wished to vindicate their political stance. 'Had the advice and entreaties of MODERATE MEN been attended to', they argued, 'the constitution and administration of the country would now be secure'.

80 John Gillies (1747–1836), *The History of Ancient Greece, its colonies, its conquests; from the earliest accounts till the division of the Macedonian in the East* (first published 1786). Gillies, Glasgow educated, wrote with a strong Whig bias.

81 'Junius' was the pen name for the author of a series of political letters that first appeared in late 1760s. These political articles, with a Whig stance, took up the causes of John Wilkes and the freedom of the press, attacked the government's Irish policy and were critical of George III. They are said to have been influenced by Bolingbroke, Swift and Tacitus. The identity of the writer has never been confirmed but those at some time suspected included Wilkes himself, Edmund Burke, Lord Chatham and Henry Flood. The most likely author appears to have been the Irish-born Sir Philip Francis (1740–1818), one of the founders of the Society for the Friends of the People.

82 There is no clue here as to the identity of this 'celebrated historian'.

83 Note here that the authors are, in this case, reluctant to include themselves in the 'moderate' bracket, when it is associated with anything like indifference or inaction in the cause of reform.

84 Tacitus (*c.*AD 56–117), Roman historian. He was a critic of concentration of power in the hands of emperors but feared civil war and anarchy as worse extremes. Pliny, 'the Elder' (AD 23–79), Roman historian and scientist, famed for his advanced techniques of observation. Cato 'the Younger' (95–46 BC), opponent of the triumvirate and, like Cicero, one of the last defenders of the Roman republic.

85 This was the first in a series of two essays which appeared in the *Belfast News-Letter* on Parliamentary reform on 15 and 19 Feb. It was a summary of the various plans for Parliamentary reform composed by some of the most prominent reformers in late eighteenth-century British politics. For this period, see A. Burns and J. Inness (eds), *Rethinking the Age of Reform, 1780–1850* (Cambridge, 2003). When the 15 Feb. essay was printed, the *News-Letter* also revealed that the Irish

House of Commons was resolving itself into a committee to consider the issue of reform. Ominously, the newspaper also contained news that the French National Assembly had declared war against Britain and the United States of Holland.

86   This is from Locke's *Two Treatises of Government*, Book II, chapter 13.

87   Henry Grattan (1740–1820), leader of the Irish Parliamentary patriot party. Nineteenth-century nationalists dubbed the period from 1782 to 1800 'Grattan's Parliament' because of his prominence in the move for legislative independence. See R. B. McDowell, *Grattan: A Life* (Dublin, 2001).

88   William Pitt, 'the Elder' (1708–78).

89   Charles Lennox, third Duke of Richmond (1735–1806). Radical Whig and one of the founders of the late eighteenth-century Parliamentary reform movement. For his long-standing involvement with the Irish Volunteers, see *A Letter from His Grace, the Duke of Richmond, To Lieutenant Colonel Sharman, Chairman to the Committee of Correspondence appointed by the Delegates of forty-five Corps of Volunteers, assembled at Lisburn in Ireland with notes by A Member of the Society of Constitutional Information* (London, 1792). He opposed the Union of 1800 because he thought it was not a 'union of hearts, hands, of affections and interests' (*DNB*).

90   Dr Richard Price (1767–90). Welsh nonconformist moral philosopher and political radical, with links to Benjamin Franklin and Thomas Jefferson. He was friends with Joy and had discussed the Catholic question with him since the early 1780s. See Price to Joy, 23 Sept. 1783, *Joy MSS* 11. 'In abstract theory', Price believed the Catholics deserved full emancipation, including the right to sit in Parliament but at that time doubted whether such a measure was 'prudent or safe'. 'This, therefore, makes one instance in which the principles of liberty cannot in practice be carried their full length'.

91   Rev. Christopher Wyvill (1740–1822) of the Yorkshire Association. For his interest in Irish affairs and his involvement with the Belfast Committee of Volunteers, see *A Collection of Letters on the proposed reformation of the Parliament of Ireland containing the first letter of the Committee of Belfast to the Rev. Christopher Wyvill: and all the letters which have been addressed to him by that committee to which is prefixed his address to the freeholders of Yorkshire* (York, 1783).

92   Dr John Jebb (1736–86). Dublin born reformer based at Cambridge University. See *Letters addressed to the Volunteers of Ireland, on the subject of a parliamentary reform* (London, 1786).

93   Thomas Howard, Earl of Effingham (1746–91). Another prominent reformer and correspondent of the Belfast Committee of Volunteers.

94   Scot and lot was a tax which contributed to local municipal expenses, such as relief of the poor. Before the 1832 Reform Act, in some boroughs the right to vote was restricted to scot and lot payers.

95   Major John Cartwright (1740–1821). Lincolnshire squire, known as the 'Father of Reform'. Founder of the Society for Constitutional Information, one of the foremost instruments of the late eighteenth-century reform movement. He welcomed the French Revolution but was critical of Painite radicalism.

96   The Dungannon meeting of 1783 took place at the height of the strength of the Volunteer movement, the year after the extension of legislative independence had been granted to the Irish parliament. The work of the Ulster Committee of Correspondence had been to build on that success by forging links with the wider British Parliamentary reform movement.

97   Potwalloper boroughs were generally boroughs in which most male householders and lodgers could vote. The term referred to anyone who had a hearth on which to boil (wallop) a pot, thus qualifying them for a vote.

98   This Number, appearing in the *News-Letter* on 19 Feb. 1793 was a continuation of the previous essay of 15 Feb. That Nos. IX and X appeared at the same time as the 1793 Convention of Volunteers is no coincidence. The plans of reform which they reproduced – an amalgam of Wyvill, Cartwright, Price and others – represent an attempt to redirect the Volunteers down a more traditional path. The points of the plans in themselves would have been uncontroversial to the bulk of Volunteer and Whig reformers for the last decade; they call for abolition of placemen and government pensions, reform of rotten boroughs and more frequent Parliamentary elections. The difference between the various plans rarely amount to much more than quibbles about the ballot, the amount of property required to vote or the frequency of elections (for the attitude of the Irish Parliamentary Whigs party to reform in the preceding years see N. Herman, 'The Irish Whigs and popular politics, 1789–92', in R. Gillespie (ed.), *The Making of Modern Ireland, 1750–1950: Beckett Prize Essays in Irish History* (Dublin, 2004), pp. 49–71). More significant is what they omitted from this account. It seems that the authors were trying to marginalise the agenda of the United Irishmen, some of whom had begun to countenance the possibility of a more radical, democratic reform of the representation on the principles of universal manhood suffrage. By late December 1792, the Dublin Society of United Irishmen had voted by a small majority to reject property qualifications as a condition for the exercise of the franchise (see Curtin, *United Irishmen*, pp. 24–5).

99   This was the last Volunteer convention of the 1780s.

100 Sir William Blackstone (1723–80), jurist, Professor of Common Law at Oxford, author of *Commentaries on the Laws of England* (1765–69). He was a foremost exponent of the common law tradition and its centrality to the British constitution.

101 This is a reference to Prime Minister William Pitt 'the Younger' (1759–1806). Although he was not seen as such a committed a reformer as his father, Lord Chatham, Pitt did periodically introduce moderate measures of reform for discussion in Parliament. His 1785 Bill proposed an abolition of 36 rotten boroughs and a moderate redistribution of seats. After it was defeated, he was criticised for not staking his premiership on the issue and this was his last attempt at such a measure.

102 Henry Flood (1732–91), Irish patriot leader with close links to the Volunteers. He was often overshadowed by the more prominent figure of Henry Grattan.

103 No. XI was an addition to the previous two Numbers and it did not appear in the original series of *Belfast News-Letter* essays. It discusses the progress of the reform movement in the interval from the time when the essays were first printed until *Belfast Politics* was published.

104 This society was formed in the King's Inn Tavern in Dublin on 21 Dec. 1792 as part of the moderate Whig response to the United Irishmen. It was largely composed of MPs from the Irish patriot party with the Whig grandee, the Duke of Leinster, as the president. The author of the plan is not cited but it may have been George Ponsonby who was a key figure in pushing the cause of reform in the Irish Parliament in the first half of the 1790s.

105 This plan of reform is not attributed to any source and seems to be the authors' personal summary of the various plans listed in the previous Number. In calling for a rationalisation of electoral districts and a franchise based on property qualifications it does not depart much from the general thrust of the reform plans listed in No. X. Indeed, aside from rejecting universal suffrage, the authors appear flexible on the property qualification and generally ready to compromise: 'There will probably be much variety of opinion on the question of qualification from property'. For this attempt to find a common ground, see No. XII.

106 Not included in the original essays, this was the most recent plan of reform to go before the Irish House of Commons when the authors of *Belfast Politics* went to press. Ponsonby's Bill was supported by Henry Grattan who spoke against borough-mongering and ministerial corruption. But the Irish Whigs, in accordance with the views of Bruce and Joy, also took the opportunity to attack manhood suffrage which was the main feature of the plan of reform recently published by that 'blasted Jacobin Society', the Dublin United Irishmen. It was defeated at the end of the 1794 session by 142 to 44 votes and reflected the increasing impotence of Parliamentary Whigs in the 1790s. See McDowell, *Grattan*, pp. 121–3, 140–68.

107 Although this essay is undated in the text, it appeared in the *News-Letter* on 15 Mar. 1793. It was printed in the wake of a military riot in Belfast of which the *News-Letter* was extremely critical. The response of the moderates in this case, was to plea for all those interested in reform to 'unite their endeavours'. As in the previous Number, there is an emphasis on the existing consensus on issues such as rotten boroughs and Ministerial corruption (see N. Herman, 'The Irish Whigs and popular politics, 1789–92', in Gillespie (ed.), *Making of Modern Ireland*, pp. 49–71). Also, as in Nos X and XI, the authors show willingness to compromise on the precise terms of any future property quali-fications. But there is a clear line on reform beyond which the authors will not go; the underpinning theme of this essay is the rejection of universal suffrage, a clear rebuke to the United Irishmen. '"Civil Liberty", when pursued to an extreme, like every other extreme, like every other extreme, may merge into its opposite, into despotism'.

108 Sir William Blackstone (1723–80), jurist, Professor of Common Law at Oxford, author of *Commentaries on the Laws of England* (1765–9).

109 The *Belfast News-Letter* of 5 Apr. 1793 also printed a copy of the military proclamation of Belfast. Joy's editorial on that occasion, along with this essay, amounted to the clearest exposition of the moderate position. The behaviour of the government and the suspension of the rule of law showed just how much had been lost from the 'venerable system of our Gothic ancestors'. But readers were also reminded, that under no other system were liberties so 'amply secure'. The French Revolution, as this essay argued, afforded 'an instructive lesson in politics' to both government (of the dangers of ignoring public opinion) and radicals (given the reports of continued faction fighting and anarchy in Paris). Notably, for the first time, Joy claimed that he had received suggestions from readers that 'Thoughts on the British Constitution' should be collected and printed as a whole.

110 The Declaration of the Rights of Man, 6 Aug. 1789, declared the natural liberty and equality of all men, guaranteed the rights of the individual (including the sanctity of property), abolished aris-tocratic privilege and limited royal power. It was essentially the manifesto of the French Revolution.

111 Nidus, the central point or locus of an organism or a nest in which spiders deposit their eggs. The authors were referring to the prominent involvement of men of Ulster Presbyterian background in the struggle for American independence. For a brief and sceptical account of this involvement, see K. Kenny, *The American Irish: A History* (New York, 2000), pp. 38–41.

112 The Edict of Nantes, which granted French Protestants substantial toleration, was issued in 1598 by King Henry IV to draw a line under the long-running religious wars in France. But it was revoked in 1685 by Louis XIV, leading to an exodus of Protestants from France, which included some of Joy's Huguenot ancestors.

113 Letters with the royal seal of the King of France. These were effectively legislative acts, which were often used to incarcerate political opponents.

114 Madame de Maintenon (1635–1719) had been governess to Louis XIV's children, before marrying him. She was often thought to influence much of his decision making, particularly the persecution of Protestants.

115 Madame Pompadour, became Louis XV's mistress. Another lady thought to have had an undue influence on a French King.

116 Hugues de Latude (1725–1805). Renegade Parisian bookseller imprisoned in the Bastille.

117 This seems to refer to the work of Irish born traveller and writer Lawrence Sterne (1713–68), *A Sentimental Journey through France and Italy* (1768).

118 Theseus was a legendary king of Athens who travelled to Crete to kill the Minotaur. On his return to Athens he forgot to hoist the white sails which should have been used to assure those waiting for the ship of his survival. According to legend, this caused his father, Aegeus, to assume he was dead and leap to his death in despair. Theseus sat in the chair of forgetfulness in Hell.

119 Phalaris of Acragas (*c.*570–549 BC), Sicilian tyrant and a by-word in antiquity for cruelty. Cacus was known in Greek mythology as a savage fire-breathing monster who inhabited the Palatine and terrorised the surrounding countryside.

120 Louis Brulart de Sillery (1737–93), minister to Louis XV.

121 This refers to an assassination attempt in 1757 when a man called Damiens stabbed the King in the side of his body with a penknife.

122 A Janizary was a soldier of the privileged French military class.

123 Jaques Neckar, French finance minister before the French Revolution. Under popular pressure in 1787, Louis XVI reappointed him as director-general of finances and minister of state. Neckar was seen as a moderate reformer and it was his dismissal in 1789 that sparked the storming of the Bastille.

124 Seigneurs were French landlords in the pre-Revolutionary feudal system.

125 Gabelles were French land taxes. Corvee referred to a feudal law to designate unpaid labour due from tenants to their land.

126 Dungannon was the town where the Ulster Volunteer conventions traditionally took place. See introduction.

127 The authors seem to have made a mistake in the dating of this issue in the text. It originally appeared as No. VIII in the *News-Letter* series on 5 Feb. 1793. Clearly they thought that it fitted into the sequence of essays more appropriately here but the context in which it first appeared was significant. 'On the eve of a war' with France, the essay was originally a response to the government's attempt to suppress the Volunteer movement.

128 Edward Wortley Montagu (1713–76), traveller, one time MP for Huntingdon and writer of *Reflections on the rise and fall of the ancient republicks, adapted to the present state of Great Britain* (London, 1759).

129 Game laws were statutes that imposed regulations of income and landholding in the right to hunt and poach in the country. Strengthened in 1671 to make these activities the exclusive preserve of landed wealth, they were a standard source of radical grievance from the 1770s because of the belief that they jettisoned ancient rights in the interests of the most privileged social groups. For example, see E. P. Thompson, *Whigs and Hunters: The Origin of the Black Act* (London, 1975).

130 Rotuli Parliamentorum – Parliamentary proceedings.

131 The *Belfast News-Letter* of 12 Apr. 1793 was dominated by news from the Continent, in particular the momentary retreat of the French army from the Low Countries. In the context of

full-scale European war, this Number reflects back wistfully on the early 'pacific declarations' of the French Republic and the instability of the republican form of government.

132 John Gillies (1747–1836). This refers to his 1778 work, *The Orations of Lysias and Isocrates*.

133 In the first few years of the Revolution the French revolutionaries had made largely conciliatory gestures to other European states. This changed with the 19 Nov. 1792 'Edict of Fraternity' which called on people all over Europe to overthrow their rulers with the help of the French and the 31 Jan. 1793 declaration which claimed France's 'natural frontiers' extended to the Rhine, Alps and Pyrennes. On 1 Feb. 1793 France declared war on Britain, Spain and the United Provinces.

134 This refers to the Orchakov Affair of 1791, when Pitt – with Prussian prompting – had considered going to war to prevent further Russian expansion at the expense of the Ottoman Empire. In the face of great Parliamentary opposition Pitt had been forced into an embarrassing retreat over the issue and called an uneasy truce with Catherine II. See J. Ehrman, *The Younger Pitt: The Reluctant Transition* (London, 1983), pp. 3–41.

135 Edward Wortley Montagu (1713–76), one time MP for Huntingdon and writer of *Reflections on the rise and fall of the ancient republicks, adapted to the present state of Great Britain* (London, 1759).

136 On 30 Apr. 1793, the *Belfast News-Letter* contained reports of further political faction fighting and instability in Paris. As Marat called on the Jacobins to crush the government of Dumouriez, Joy's editorial pointed to this Number as evidence of the 'curious coincidence between the French Republic and that of Athens, in so much that the latter would seem to have been the model of the former in many striking points'.

137 Anacharsis was a legendary Scythian prince and philosopher. It was believed that he became a Greek citizen, before returning to his own people with the intention of instructing them in the ways of the Greeks. However, he also extolled the simple life of the Scythians and was later seen as exemplifying the barbarian critique of Greek customs.

138 This is most likely a reference to Thomas Paine or perhaps William Godwin. For the attitudes of Bruce and Joy to these thinkers, see the editor's introduction.

139 Attica was the surrounding territory of Athens – though it is sometimes used to refer to Athens itself – separated from the rest of the Greek mainland by a mountain range.

140 In May 1790, the government of Paris was reorganised into 48 local administrative 'sections'.

141 Demarchs were elected by lot and were in general expected to play the role of impartial magistrates or officials.

142 Aristides 'the Just' (530–468 BC), Athenian politician who was held up by Plutarch as a man of great integrity and dignity, who treated everyone with impartiality and a sense of justice.

143 By the French Constitution of 1790 the Provinces of France were abolished and divided into departments, each provided with a local administration.

144 In 1790, the French insurrectionists deposed the traditional government of Paris and installed in its place an executive council.

145 The Legislative Assembly, composed of 750 members, replaced the Constituent Assembly as the legislative authority of France in October 1791.

146 Solon (d. 559 BC), Athenian poet and politician. Referred to by Plutarch as the 'lawmaker of Athens', he was seen as a hero by Athenian democrats and is usually credited with strengthening the rights of the Athenian assembly against the powers of the noble families.

147 This again refers to Anacharsis, legendary Scythian prince and philosopher.

148 Areopagus is used to refer to the 'Hill of Acres' at Athens and the ancient council, or court, which was named after it. It was the Areopagus that elected the nine 'archons' who ruled Athens. Before the reforms of Solon, the membership of this council was almost exclusively aristocratic.

149 The *euthynai* was the examination of accounts which every public official underwent when he had completed his office. Le Bureau de Comptabilité performed a similar function in Revolutionary France.

150 Jean Jacques Barthelemi (1716–95). He was the highly esteemed French author of *The Travels of Anacharsis the Younger in Greece* which appeared in France in 1788. It was said to have had great impact on philhellenism in France in the years before the Revolution, by making the work of Anacharsis accessible to those who were unfamiliar with ancient languages. Bathelemi fell out of favour after the Revolution and died in prison in 1795.

151 Codrus, the King of Athens in the eleventh century BC. According to legend, he selflessly gave up his life to the invading Dorian army in order to save his people.

152 Pisistratus, tyrant of Athens, ruled for 36 years before dying in 527BC. He seized control from the divided political factions in Athens and imposed a strong rule military rule.

153 Cleon was an Athenian politician active in the fifth century BC, seen as one of a new brand of politician who had to rely on oratory and demagogy for political survival rather than aristocratic breeding. He was seen as a very effective speaker, prone to extravagant promises and wild accusations against opponents. Alcibiades was another flamboyant Athenian politician, active in the same period. As an aristocrat he is said to have competed with this new brand of politician by recourse to similar methods; he was noted in particular for his personal ambition and use of intrigue. By contrast, Themistocles (*c.*524–459 BC) was a politician whose virtue and far-sightedness is admired in the writings of Thucydides. Aristides 'the Just' was also known for typifying aristocratic virtue against demagogy and misrepresentation.

154 Conon, Iphicrates, Timotheus, Chabrias and Nepos (to whom this account is attributed) were all Greek soldiers or generals active in the fourth and fifth centuries BC and who spent most of their lives away from Athens, partly through military campaigns, partly by choice.

155 Sallust (*c.*86–35 BC), Roman tribune and distinguished historian.

156 This refers to a naval battle of the Peloponnesian War fought among the Arginuse islands in 406 BC. The Athenian commander, Conon, destroyed 70 or 120 enemy ships and killed his opposing commander. However, when a storm arose after the battle and drowned many of the Athenian sailors on their damaged ships, eight out of the top ten Athenian officers were exiled or executed.

157 The Peloponnesian war was fought between Sparta and Athens between 431 and 404 BC. The authors most likely gained their knowledge of this from Thucydides' *The History of the Peloponnesian War* (*c.* 431BC).

158 The 'faction of the four hundred' emerged in 411 BC during the crisis caused by the Peloponnesian wars. Athenian democracy was overthrown and the four hundred were granted powers to revise the constitution on a more economical basis. With continued Athenian failure in the war, this arrangement lasted only four months.

159 The 'thirty tyrants' were a pro-Spartan oligarchy, installed in Athens after defeat by Sparta in 404 BC. They reduced the number of Athenian citizens and curtailed many of their rights.

160 Aristophanes (c.448–380 BC), one of the most famous comics of Ancient Greece, writing during the Peloponnesian wars.

161 Phocion (402–318 BC), Athenian statesman and general. He was renowned as an incorruptible and independent political thinker. But after negotiating terms for Athens in the wake of defeat by the Macedonian kings, he was condemned to death during the brief democratic revolution of Polyphercon (318 BC).

162 Philip of Macedon completed his great victory over the Athenians and their allies in 338 BC and subsequently took control of most of Greece.

163 *The Spirit of the Laws*, Book I, chapter 16.

164 This section did not appear in the original *Belfast News-Letter* essay. It seems to have been added as a postscript, coinciding with the new French Revolutionary calendar which came into existence in that month. By this system, the year began on 22 September (of the Christian calendar) and was divided into twelve months of thirty days. Each month was divided into three weeks, called decades.

165 Demetrius Poliorcetes (*c.*337–283BC), King of Macedon and legendary warrior.

166 This essay appeared in the *Belfast News-Letter* of 1 Nov. 1793. The issue was dominated by the execution of Marie Antoinette, Queen of France. The original essay was unusually long so in the book the authors split it into it Nos XVII and XVIII.

167 This is most likely a quotation from Tacitus Livy (*c.*59 BC–AD17). His *History of Rome* was still very influential in the eighteenth century. Before Livy, most Roman historians had written in Greek, as it was seen as the language of culture. This quotation, in Latin, fits his admiration for the civilisation of early Rome. The use of Livy here also supports Quentin Skinner's argument for the importance of the neo-Roman dimension of the republican understanding of liberty. See *Liberty Before Liberalism* (Cambridge, 1997).

168 Note here, the use of 'writers' suggests that the text had a shared authorship between Bruce and Joy.

169 The specific complaint of the moderates was that at the trial of the King in Paris, the revolutionary authorities had 'joined the judicial with the legislative power . . . which can never be joined without tyranny, they were the accusers and the evidence' (*Belfast News-Letter*, 5 Feb. 1793).

170 The Constitutions of Clarendon were introduced by Henry II in 1164 in order to settle the relations between Church and State and to subject the clergy to the full legal process; the laws of Edward the Confessor were thought to contain some of the most important Anglo-Saxon rights and privileges, jeopardised by the Conquest; 'the institution of circuits' refers to the introduction of itinerary royal courts functioning throughout England in regular circuits.

171 The 'provisions of Oxford' were a scheme of government reform forced on Henry III by his barons, led by Simon de Montfort, angry at the King's costly foreign adventures. A council of fifteen was established to advise the King and meet three times a year in order to scrutinise his spending and taxation. These later became known as the Westminster provision.

172 In 1327, Parliament met at Westminster to declare that Edward III would take over as King, his father having been deposed.

173 Henry VI was the youngest king ever to ascend to the throne of England. The 'minority' refers to the period of his reign (1422–37) before he came of age to govern as King himself, when the country was run by a group of lords and retainers ('Protectors').

174 James I was a staunch exponent of the 'divine right of Kings' theory and he clashed regularly with Parliament over what they saw as his extravagant expenditure on foreign affairs.

175 These disputes were instrumental in the run up to the English Civil War (1642–51). The Star Chamber was the ancient meeting place of the King's ministers but it came to be seen as a vehicle for extending the royal prerogative and was abolished by the Long Parliament in 1640. The Court of High Commission, which handled ecclesiastical issues, was also a focal point of grievance and was abolished with the Star Chamber. Ship money was a seaport tax which Charles I had tried to levy across the country in 1635, leading to vociferous opposition.

176 The Act of Toleration of 1689 granted a significant level of toleration to Dissenters. The Bill of Rights of the same year confirmed the Declaration of Rights which had been presented to William and Mary on their arrival in England, following the abdication of James II. It secured many ancient English rights and recited the abuses of the royal prerogative which had taken place in James II's reign.

177 The Test Act of 1673 required all office holders in the state, including MPs, to take the communion of the Church of England every year. The Acts of Uniformity (1549, 1552, 1559, 1662) enforced the use of the Book of Common Prayer in all religious services.

178 For a deeper discussion of these, see No. XIX

179 These were the provisions of Charles James Fox's celebrated 1792 Libel Bill.

180 These acts are discussed in much more detail in No. XIX.

181 For the increasingly muted and ineffective Irish Parliamentary opposition to the government's campaign of repression in the 1790s, see N. Curtin, '"A perfect liberty"', pp. 270–89.

182 See Essay No. XIX.

183 Ibid.

184 This is a continuation of the last Number, the second half of the essay which appeared in the *Belfast News-Letter* on 1 Nov. 1793. The quotations from Montesquieu were not in the original.

185 It is not clear to whom the author is referring here. He may have had in mind the Stewart family of County Down. By the late eighteenth century they were increasingly accepted into the circles of the Anglican ruling elite, while remaining conscious of their Presbyterian dissent. The young Robert Stewart, later Lord Castlereagh, was fast emerging as one of the leading men in the Irish Parliament.

186 This phrase was originally from Cicero's *In Verrem*. I owe this point to Dr Michael Brown.

187 This refers to a classical anecdote in which Tarquin, one of the Kings of Rome, would proceed up and down his garden, lopping off the heads of the tallest poppies with his staff.

188 William Godwin (1756–1836) is known as the founder of philosophical anarchism. *An Enquiry Concerning Political Justice* (1793) argued that government was a corrupting force in society. See, I. Kramnick, 'On anarchism and the real world: William Godwin and radical England', *American Political Science Review* 66, 1 (Mar. 1972), pp. 114–28; F. Rosen, *Progress and Democracy: William Godwin's Contribution to Political Philosophy* (New York and London, 1987). Godwin was very much of the new, post-Paine breed of radical that regarded old notions such as constitutional checks and balances as spurious and a mask for corruption. With Henry Yorke, he regarded the idea of a constitution that served as a set of checks against groups with different interests, rather than as a servant of the common interest, as a 'blasphemy against human nature' (see Worden, *Roundhead Reputations*, pp. 210–11).

189 Antaeus, in Greek mythology, was a giant and a wrestler. He was made stronger every time he was thrown to the ground, through contact with his mother, the Earth. Hydra was a snake with many heads. Every time one of these was cut off, it grew several more in its place.

190 This Number appeared on 8 Nov. 1793, in an addition of the *Belfast News-Letter* which was dominated by the intensification of military hostilities on the Continent. The quotations from Hume were added at a later date.

191 This quotation is from David Hume's 'Liberty of the press' in his *Essays, Moral, Political and Literary*, Part I, Essay 2 (1742).

192 Poyning's law (10. Hen,. VII, cc. 9, 11, Dec. 1493) was the central focus of Irish patriot grievances. In 1494, Sir Henry Poyning, acting on behalf of the King, summoned the Irish Parliament to Drogheda. There it was made more subservient to the English one, and could not be summoned or pass laws without English consent.

193 Barry Yelverton's Act (21 & 22 Geo. III, c. 47, July 1782) amended Poyning's law and was regarded as a great success for the Irish patriot party. Broadly speaking, this empowered the Irish Parliament to propose legislation itself and removed the power of the Irish Privy Council to block or amend that legislation.

194 William Molyneux (1656–98) was greatly influenced by the work of Locke, with whom he was well acquainted. He challenged the right of England to legislate for Ireland, particularly the negative effect it had on the wool industry. Interestingly, Molyneux also mooted a union between Britain and Ireland as a potential solution to these problems. For discussion of a union among early Irish patriots and Molyneux's indebtedness to Locke, see C. Robbins, *The Eighteenth-Century Commonwealthman: Studies in the Transmission, Development and Circumstances of English Liberal Thought from the Restoration of Charles II and the War with Thirteen Colonies* (Cambridge, Mass., 1959), pp. 135–43. See also, J. Kelly, 'Public and political opinion in Ireland before the idea of an Anglo-Irish Union', in Boyce et al. (eds), *Political Discourse*, pp. 110–41. For Molyneux's continued influence in the eighteenth century, see P. Kelly, 'William Molyneux and the spirit of liberty in eighteenth-century Ireland', *Eighteenth-Century Ireland* 3 (1998), pp. 133–48.

195 In October 1719, the Irish House of Lords presented a petition to the Lord Lieutenant, for submission to the King, protesting against the behaviour of the British House of Lords.

196 See I. Victory, 'The making of the Declaratory Act of 1720', in G. O'Brien (ed.), *Parliament, Politics and People: Essays in Eighteenth-Century Irish History* (Dublin, 1989), pp. 9–30. This declared that the Irish parliament was 'subordinate unto and dependent upon' the King and Parliament of England. The Act, repealed in 1782, had undermined traditional Anglo-Irish notions of political legitimacy, rooted in notions of inheritance of common law rights. Victory argues that this saw a departure from the defence of Irish rights on the basis of historical, judicial and legislative precedents and led to a new, Lockean emphasis on natural right.

197 Jonathan Swift (1667–1745), Dean of St Patrick's Cathedral, Dublin and author of *Gulliver's Travels* (1726). Another important Irish patriot figure, his *Drapier's Letters* (1724) challenged the right of England to introduce a debased coinage in Ireland called 'Wood's ha'pence'. Lord John Carteret, Lord Lieutenant from 1724 to 1730, had a strong personal liking for Swift and in 1725 he announced the withdrawal of 'Wood's ha'pence'.

198 In December 1753, the Irish House of Commons rejected a Bill to apply the Irish revenue surplus to the reduction of the British national debt.

199 John Wilkes (1725–98), radical MP for Middlesex. He was a leading critic of George III and the government of Lord Bute and in 1762 he set up a journal called *The North Briton* to attack the government. Warrants were soon issued for the arrest of the printers and writers of *The North*

Briton. This caused a political storm because they were seen to contravene habeas corpus and Wilkes's Parliamentary privilege and became a test case for freedom of the press.

200 Octennial Act (7 Geo. III, c. 3, 16 Feb. 1768).

201 The first company of Belfast Volunteers enrolled on 17 March 1778.

202 The Catholic Relief Act (17 & 18 Geo. III, c. 49, 14 Aug. 1778) enabled Catholics to take leases for 999 years and gave them the same inheritance laws as Protestants.

203 In November 1779 the Volunteers paraded in Dublin, demanding relief from commercial restrictions. The Irish Commons subsequently passed a motion extending Ireland's right to free trade, while guaranteeing continued access to the British Imperial market.

204 Barry Yelverton's Act (21 & 22 Geo. III, c. 47, July 1782) amended Poyning's law and was regarded as a great success for the Irish patriot party. Broadly speaking, this empowered the Irish parliament to propose legislation itself and removed the power of the Irish Privy Council to block or amend that legislation.

205 Catholic Relief Act (21&22 Geo. III, c. 24, 4 May 1782), allowed Catholics to acquire land, except in Parliamentary Boroughs.

206 Catholic Relief Act (21&22 Geo. III, c. 50, 27 July 1782) allowed Catholics to teach in school and act as guardians; Protestant Dissenter Relief Act (21&22 Geo. III, c. 25, 4 May 1782) declared the validity of Presbyterian marriages; Protestant Dissenters Relief Act (21&22 Geo. III, c. 57, 27 July 1782) exempted Seceders from kissing the Bible when taking oaths.

207 Independency of Judges Act (21&22 Geo. III, c. 50).

208 George Forbes (1760–1837), later sixth Earl Granard. Another Irish patriot politician, he was a co-founder, with Grattan, Ponsonby and Lord Charlemont, of the Dublin Whig Club in 1790.

209 On 12 May 1785, Pitt spoke in the House of Commons, modifying his commercial propositions (for freeing trade between Britain and Ireland) following vociferous opposition in Ireland.

210 The *Belfast News-Letter* of 12 Nov. was again dominated by the war on the Continent and the continued faction fighting among the French revolutionaries, leading to the trial of Brissot and other condemned deputies.

211 Sir John St Aubyn, third baronet (1700–44), MP for Cornwall and opponent of Walpole's government. He won the reputation of being an upright politician who could not be corrupted or bribed.

212 For the fortunes of the Parliamentary Whig campaign for reform in these years, see McDowell, *Grattan*, pp. 140–69.

213 This is clearly a critique of the political tactics of the United Irishmen.

214 The Place Act (33 Geo. III, c. 29, 16 Aug. 1793) disqualified holders of certain government offices and pensions from membership of the House of Commons.

215 Another reference to Fox's Libel Bill. Lord Camden (1714–94), who held office in Pitt's administration, was instrumental in seeing the Libel Bill through the House of Lords in 1792. One of his main opponents in the Lords had been Lord Mansfield (1705–93), famous for his involvement in numerous cases of libel law.

216 Tithes for the benefit of the Episcopalian Church were a mainstay of Catholic and Presbyterian grievance until the Whig reforms of the 1830s.

217 The Catholic Relief Act (33 Geo. III, c. 2, 9 Apr. 1793) extended Parliamentary franchise to Catholics, enabling them to hold most civil and military offices, and removing the statutory bar to

university degrees. Within two years the Roman Catholic seminary at Maynooth had been established by the Irish Parliament (35 Geo. III, c. 21, 5 June 1795).

218 The Convention Act (33 Geo. III, c. 29, 16 Aug. 1793) outlawed assemblies which purported to represent the people by preparing petitions for King or Parliament. As both radicals and moderates later complained, this had the effect of driving the reform movement under ground.

219 The Gunpowder Act (33 Geo. III, c. 2, 25 Feb. 1793) prevented the importation of arms and ammunition and their movement without licence. This was of great offence to the civic humanist sensibilities of even the most moderate of Volunteers. The right to bear arms was regarded as one of the most important liberties secured by the British Constitution.

220 Henry Flood (1732–91), Irish patriot leader with close links to the Volunteers. He was often overshadowed by the more prominent figure of Henry Grattan.

221 See n. 81 above.